ORIENTAL COOKERY

ORIENTAL COOKERY

KENNETH LO & TERRY TAN

First published in Great Britain in 1988.
This edition published in 1996 by Hamlyn
an imprint of Reed Consumer Books Limited
Michelin House, 81 Fulham Road, London SW3 6RB
and Auckland, Melbourne, Singapore and Toronto

ISBN 0 600 58952 8

Produced by Mandarin Offset
Printed in Hong Kong

CONTENTS

SOUPS

Oriental soups contain many unusual combinations of foods and flavourings. Several soups here have meats, flavoured with a variety of herbs and spices. There is one with dumplings and one – Stuffed squid soup – where the squid is stuffed with minced pork. The result is delicious and decidedly exotic.

Fresh and dried shrimp soup with spinach and bean curd (see page 10)

CELEBRATION DUMPLING SOUP

3 tablespoons oil
4 garlic cloves, peeled and chopped
1 litre (1¾ pints) water
1 tablespoon soy sauce
½ teaspoon pepper
200 g (7 oz) minced pork
100 g (4 oz) minced prawns
100 g (4 oz) bamboo shoots, shredded
1 teaspoon cornflour
2 teaspoons salt
1 tablespoon chopped spring onions

Preparation time: 15 minutes
Cooking time: 10 minutes

This is a festive dish, served during Chinese New Year or on other important occasions. You could vary the flavour by substituting crab meat for the prawns. Any bamboo shoot shreds not mixed into the dumplings can be left loose in the soup to impart a distinctive flavour. Meat or chicken stock, instead of water, will make the soup even richer, and fresh coriander makes a fragrant garnish.
1. Heat the oil in a frying pan or wok and fry the garlic till golden brown. Remove, drain and divide into two lots.
2. Bring the water to the boil in a saucepan and add the soy sauce and pepper.
3. Combine all the remaining ingredients, except half the fried garlic. Mix well and shape into balls, each the size of a walnut.
4. Place the dumpling balls in the boiling water and simmer for 8 minutes, tasting and adjusting the seasoning, if necessary.
5. Serve the soup hot with a topping of fried garlic and more pepper, if you like.

HOT AND SOUR SLICED LIVER SOUP WITH BEAN CURD

SERVES 4–5 with 1 or 2 other dishes
225 g (8 oz) lamb's liver
1 teaspoon salt
1 teaspoon vegetable oil
100 g (4 oz) celery sticks
1½ tablespoons cornflour
1 cake Chinese or Japanese bean curd
1.2 litres (2 pints) chicken stock
4 tablespoons light soy sauce
2 chicken stock cubes
5 tablespoons vinegar
3 tablespoons freshly ground chopped
    spring onions
½ teaspoon black pepper
2 teaspoons sesame oil
1 tablespoon chopped watercress

Preparation time: 15 minutes, plus standing
Cooking time: 10 minutes

This is a useful soup because it is so easy to make, and it is very warming in winter, too. Other meats may be substituted for the lamb's liver, if you like.
1. Cut the liver into thin strips, about 2 × 1 cm (1 × ½ inch). Place in a dish, sprinkle with salt and oil and leave to stand for 1 hour. Clean the celery and cut it into 3 cm (1½ inch) pieces. Blend the cornflour with 4–5 tablespoons water to make a smooth paste. Cut the bean curd into 12 cubes.
2. Heat the stock in a large saucepan. When hot add the soy sauce, celery, bean curd and crumbled stock cubes and leave to simmer gently for 5 minutes.
3. Add the liver, vinegar, spring onion and pepper, stir and cook gently for a further 3 minutes, then stir in the blended cornflour. Continue to cook gently, stirring, for 1 minute.
4. Sprinkle the soup with sesame oil and watercress and serve in individual bowls, or in a large tureen placed in the centre of the table for the diners to help themselves.

LEFT, Celebration dumpling soup; RIGHT, Hot and sour liver soup with bean curd

FRESH AND DRIED SHRIMP SOUP WITH SPINACH AND BEAN CURD

SERVES 4–5 with 1 or 2 other dishes
3 tablespoons dried shrimps
4 slices root ginger
2 rashers bacon
150 g (5 oz) fresh spinach
1 cake Chinese or Japanese bean curd
1.5 litres (2½ pints) chicken stock
1½ teaspoons salt
1½ chicken stock cubes
150 g (5 oz) fresh or thawed peeled prawns
1 tablespoon light soy sauce
1 tablespoon vinegar
¼ teaspoon white pepper
1 tablespoon sesame oil

Preparation time: 10 minutes
Cooking time: 18 minutes

A soup of true Chinese delicacy of colouring, this has shrimps to add a fine seafood flavour.

1. Soak the dried shrimps in a cup of boiling water for 5 minutes, then drain. Cut the ginger into fine matchstick shreds. De-rind the bacon and shred it finely crossways. Wash and drain the spinach thoroughly and remove the stalks. Cut the bean curd into 18 cubes.

2. Heat the stock in a saucepan. Add the dried shrimps, bacon and ginger. Bring to the boil, then simmer gently for 10 minutes. Add the salt, crumbled stock cubes, spinach, bean curd and prawns. Slowly bring to the boil, then simmer gently for 5 minutes.

3. Add the soy sauce, vinegar, pepper and sesame oil. Stir and cook gently for a further 2 minutes, then serve in individual bowls or in a large tureen placed in the centre of the table for the diners to help themselves.

SLICED FISH AND CHINESE MUSHROOM SOUP

SERVES 4–5 with 1 or 2 other dishes
300 ml (½ pint) boiling water
8 medium Chinese dried mushrooms
225 g (8 oz) plaice or sole fillets
1 teaspoon salt
1½ tablespoons cornflour
1 egg white
about 150 ml (¼ pint) vegetable oil for shallow frying
1.5 litres (2½ pints) chicken stock
4 slices root ginger
1½ teaspoons salt
1½ chicken stock cubes
1 tablespoon vinegar
1 tablespoon light soy sauce
¾ teaspoon white pepper

Preparation time: 15 minutes, plus soaking
Cooking time: 20 minutes

This peppery soup is very popular in Peking. The nearly pure white fish and the almost black mushrooms provide an attractive contrast in colour.

1. Pour the boiling water over the dried mushrooms and leave them to soak for 30 minutes. Drain the mushrooms, retaining and straining the soaking water, and cut each cap in half. Remove and discard the stems.

2. Cut the fish into 5 × 2.5 cm (2 × 1 inch) pieces. Sprinkle the fish pieces with salt and cornflour, brush with egg white.

3. Heat the oil in a frying pan. Remove from the heat for 10 seconds and add the pieces of fish one by one, spreading them out over the pan. Return the pan to the heat and fry the fish gently for 1½ minutes, turning once. Remove the fish with a slotted spoon and drain on absorbent kitchen paper. Set aside.

4. Heat the stock in a saucepan. Add the ginger, salt, crumbled stock cubes, mushrooms and mushroom water. Bring to the boil, then simmer for 10 minutes. Add the fish, vinegar, soy sauce and pepper. Bring slowly to the boil, then simmer for 5 minutes.

5. Serve in individual bowls or in a large tureen placed in the centre of the table for the diners to help themselves.

LEFT, Sliced fish and Chinese mushroom soup; RIGHT, Fresh and dried shrimp soup with spinach and bean curd

SPARE-RIB SOUP WITH PEA-STARCH, TRANSPARENT NOODLES AND CUCUMBER

SERVES 4–5 with 1 or 2 other dishes
500 g (1¼ lb) pork spare ribs
1.5 litres (2½ pints) chicken stock
25 g (1 oz) dried shrimps
75 g (3 oz) Chinese transparent pea-starch noodles (or vermicelli noodles)
1 medium cucumber
1½ teaspoons salt
¼ teaspoon freshly ground black pepper
1½ chicken stock cubes
2 tablespoons light soy sauce
2 tablespoons chopped spring onion
1 teaspoon sesame oil

Preparation time: 15 minutes, plus soaking
Cooking time: 1 hour 50 minutes

This is a clear soup which yet manages to be rich and savoury. The inclusion of cucumber gives an extra freshness to the meaty flavour.
1. Cut the spare ribs into individual ribs, and chop each into 4 cm (1½ inch) pieces. Poach them in boiling water for 3–4 minutes. Drain and add them to a large saucepan with the stock.
2. Meanwhile, soak the dried shrimps in a cupful of boiling water for 10 minutes. Drain and add the dried shrimps to the pan with the stock and spare ribs. Bring to the boil, then simmer gently for 1½ hours.
3. Meanwhile soak the noodles in boiling water for 3 minutes, then drain and use a pair of kitchen scissors to cut the noodles into 6 cm (2½ inch) lengths. Cut the cucumber diagonally into slices, about 1 cm (½ inch) thick.
4. Add the salt, pepper, crumbled stock cubes, soy sauce and cucumber slices to the pan containing the spare ribs. Return to the boil, then simmer gently for 10 minutes. Sprinkle the top of the soup with spring onions and sesame oil.
5. Stir, simmer for a further 3–4 minutes, then serve in individual bowls or in a large tureen placed in the centre of the table for the diners to help themselves.

'SILK ROAD' LAMB GOULASH SOUP WITH LEEKS, GARLIC AND GINGER

SERVES 4–5 with 1 or 2 other dishes
750 g (1½ lb) neck of lamb
5–6 slices root ginger
3 garlic cloves
225 g (8 oz) leeks
1 tablespoon dried shrimps
75 g (3 oz) Chinese transparent pea-starch noodles (vermicelli noodles)
1.5 litres (2½ pints) chicken stock or water
1½ teaspoons salt
2 tablespoons chopped hot Szechuan (Ja Chai) pickle
1½ chicken stock cubes
1 tablespoon light soy sauce
3 tablespoons dry sherry or Chinese rice wine

Preparation time: 20 minutes, plus soaking
Cooking time: 1 hour 45 minutes

This soup takes its name from the fact that its main ingredient, lamb, is available all along the great trading route across China and central Asia and its other ingredients are easily carried on horseback or the backs of camels. It is a fine clear soup with a sharp savoury flavour.
1. Chop the lamb into 4 × 2.5 cm (1½ × 1 inch) pieces. Shred the ginger and crush the garlic. Clean the leeks and trim them, then cut them open diagonally into 4 cm (1½ inch) slices.
2. Soak the dried shrimps in a cupful of boiling water for 5 minutes, then drain. Soak the noodles in boiling water for 3 minutes, then drain. Use a pair of kitchen scissors to cut the noodles into 7.5 cm (3 inch) lengths. Parboil the lamb in sufficient water to cover for 5 minutes, then drain. Discard the water.
3. Bring the stock or water to the boil in a large saucepan or flameproof casserole. Add the lamb, ginger, garlic, salt, dried shrimps and pickle, return slowly to the boil, then simmer gently for 1½ hours.
4. Add the leeks, noodles, crumbled stock cubes, soy sauce and sherry or rice wine and simmer for a further 5 minutes. Stir, then serve in individual bowls or in a large tureen set in the centre of the table for the diners to help themselves.

FROM THE TOP, Spare-rib soup with pea-starch, transparent noodles and cucumber; 'Silk Road' lamb goulash soup with leeks, garlic and ginger

SPICY CHICKEN SOUP

3 tablespoons vegetable oil
½ large onion, peeled and thinly sliced
2 garlic cloves, peeled and crushed
1 teaspoon chopped ginger
½ teaspoon black pepper
pinch of turmeric
175 g (6 oz) chicken meat
1 litre (1¾ pints) chicken stock
1 tablespoon light soy sauce
75 g (3 oz) beansprouts
handful of beanthread noodles, soaked till soft
chopped spring onions, to garnish

Preparation time: 15–20 minutes
Cooking time: 15 minutes

Nothing from which a little stock can be coaxed is ever thrown away in an Oriental kitchen. This soup must have evolved from the ingrained sense of economy among itinerant hawkers in South-East Asia. It is the kind of soup (stock from a chicken used previously) that allows full play for your ingenuity with leftover meats, a handful of beansprouts and perhaps noodles.

1. Heat the oil and fry the onion, garlic and ginger for 2 minutes. Add the pepper, turmeric and chicken meat and stir for 30 seconds.
2. Add the stock and soy sauce and bring to the boil. Taste and adjust seasoning, if necessary. Cook for 5 minutes.
3. To serve, place a handful each of raw beansprouts and noodles in a bowl and top up with soup. Garnish with chopped spring onions. Serve a side dish of finely chopped chillies in lime juice for those who like it sharp and fiery.

STUFFED SQUID SOUP

8 medium squid
175 g (6 oz) minced pork
1 stalk spring onion, chopped
1 teaspoon salt
½ teaspoon pepper
1 teaspoon cornflour
500 ml (18 fl oz) water
1 tablespoon light soy sauce
1 tablespoon sesame oil
chopped spring onion, to garnish

Preparation time: 20 minutes
Cooking time: 10 minutes

Off the shores of Singapore, fishing stakes called 'kelongs' are an ingenious method of trapping marine creatures in an underwater fenced-in area. The enticement is not bait but the glow from swinging hurricane lamps that attracts mackerel, pomfret, whitebait and squid by the shoal. Every few hours the huge net sitting placidly on the seabed is winched up and another briny harvest is destined for the open markets in the villages.

1. Remove the tentacles from the squid by pulling them out gently. Cut off the hard gristle and eyes. Remove the sac from each squid, wash and drain. (See Cleaning Squid, page 136.)
2. Mix the minced pork with the spring onion, salt, pepper and cornflour. Stuff each squid with a little of the minced pork mixture and secure tentacles to each with a cut-off cocktail stick.
3. Set aside any leftover mixture. Bring the water to the boil and add the soy sauce and sesame oil. Add the stuffed squids and cook for 3 minutes.
4. Stir in any left-over pork mixture to give the soup 'body'. Adjust the seasoning and garnish with more chopped spring onion. Remove the cocktail sticks from the squid before serving.

LEFT, Spicy chicken soup; RIGHT, Stuffed squid soup

VEGETABLES AND SALADS

The wonderful variety of vegetables available to Oriental cooks is used in abundance in the recipes here. There are several of those extravagant combinations of fruits and vegetables known as 'great salads' and, in contrast, unusual recipes for such everyday vegetables as cabbage and marrow.

Tropical great salad (see page 34)

BRAISED CABBAGE IN SOY SAUCE

SERVES 4–5 with 1 or 2 other dishes
1.25 kg (2½ lb) Savoy cabbage
3 slices root ginger
3½ tablespoons vegetable oil
1 garlic clove, peeled and finely chopped
1 tablespoon sugar
2 tablespoons light soy sauce
1½ chicken stock cubes
4 tablespoons chicken stock
2 tablespoons dry sherry
2 tablespoons butter

Preparation time: 10–15 minutes
Cooking time: 15 minutes

This is probably the most widely cooked vegetable dish in all China. It combines freshness with savouriness and is therefore an ideal accompaniment for rice or fried rice dishes.

1. Cut the stem out of the cabbage. Cut the cabbage from the top downwards into 4–6 segments, then cut each segment into three pieces. Roughly shred the ginger.
2. Heat the oil in a large saucepan. Add the ginger and stir-fry for 30 seconds, then add the garlic and continue to stir for a further 30 seconds.
3. Add the cabbage, raise the heat and turn the cabbage in the flavoured oil. Sprinkle the cabbage with sugar, then add the sauces, crumbled stock cubes, stock and sherry. Turn the cabbage pieces around in the sauce, until they are evenly covered.

4. Add the butter, and continue to turn the cabbage for 15 seconds. Cover the pan and reduce the heat to very low. Leave to simmer gently for 10 minutes. Turn the cabbage over once more and continue to cook very gently for a further 2 minutes.

CHINESE CABBAGE WITH WHITE FU-YUNG SAUCE

SERVES 4–5 with 1 or 2 other dishes
750 g (1½ lb) Chinese cabbage
1 tablespoon dried shrimps
1 chicken stock cube
300 ml (½ pint) chicken stock

For the Fu-Yung Sauce:
2 egg whites
2 tablespoons cornflour
1 teaspoon salt
3–4 tablespoons milk
1 tablespoon cream, or
1 tablespoon butter
2 tablespoons minced chicken breast meat

Preparation time: about 10 minutes, plus soaking
Cooking time: 15 minutes

Because this dish is given a feeling of purity by its combination of the green whiteness of the Chinese cabbage and the whiteness of the Fu-Yung sauce, it is often served as a contrast to richer, dark meat dishes. It is a non-regional dish, served throughout China.

1. Cut the cabbage into 7.5 × 5 cm (3 × 2 inch) pieces. Soak the dried shrimps in boiling water for 10 minutes, then drain. Add the shrimps and crumbled stock cube to the stock in a large saucepan or deep frying-pan with a lid. Bring to the boil, stir and simmer for 1 minute.
2. Add the cabbage to the pan. Stir and mix the shrimps gently with the cabbage. Cover the pan and simmer gently for 8 minutes, stirring once or twice. Drain, reserving the cooking liquid, which will be used in the Fu–Yung sauce.

3. To make the sauce, beat the egg whites with a fork for 1 minute, then add the cornflour and salt and beat for a further 30 seconds. Add the milk, cream, butter and minced chicken then pour in the reserved stock. Stir well to mix and pour into a small saucepan. Cook, stirring over a medium heat for 2–3 minutes, until thickened.
4. Arrange the cabbage attractively in a deep serving dish. Pour the sauce evenly over.

LEFT, Braised cabbage in soy sauce; RIGHT, Chinese cabbage in white Fu-yung sauce

STIR-FRIED FRENCH BEANS WITH CHINESE DRIED SHRIMPS AND FRIED MUSHROOMS

SERVES 4–6 with 1 or 2 other dishes
450–500 g (1–1¼ lb) French beans
1½ tablespoons Chinese dried mushrooms
4–5 medium Chinese dried shrimps
4 tablespoons vegetable oil
1 tablespoon light soy sauce
1 tablespoon hoisin sauce
1 tablespoon crushed and chopped garlic
1½ tablespoons butter
1 tablespoon good stock
1½ tablespoons dry sherry

Preparation time: 8 minutes, plus blanching and soaking
Cooking time: 10 minutes

Simply cooked and often served, this dish has two dried ingredients to impart an intenser flavour to the beans by cooking them in a well-seasoned and flavoured oil over a high heat.
1. Top and tail the French beans, drop them into a pan of boiling water and blanch for 2 minutes. Drain them well.
2. Soak the mushrooms and shrimps in boiling water, for 15 minutes, then drain them. Chop the mushrooms and shrimps finely.
3. Heat the oil in a saucepan. When hot add the minced mushrooms and shrimps and cook them over a medium heat for 1½ minutes. Add the beans and stir-fry them in the oil for 2 minutes. Add the remaining ingredients to the pan. Turn the beans in the sauce so that each piece is well coated. Cover the pan and leave to cook gently for 3 minutes. Open the lid and turn and stir the ingredients once more.

4. Serve with plain boiled or steamed rice, and any brown stewed meat dishes.

Variations: For Stir-Fried Broccoli, substitute 500–750 g (1¼–1½ lb) broccoli for the beans, cut into florets, and cut away and discard the main stem, which is too thick and cannot be cooked in this manner.

For Stir-Fried Asparagus, substitute asparagus for the broccoli. Before blanching for 3 minutes, cut away and discard about 5 cm (2 inch) of the root-end of the asparagus. Cut the remaining end slantwise into three sections.

STIR-FRIED BROAD BEANS WITH PICKLED CABBAGE

½ tablespoons vegetable oil
100 g (4 oz) pickled mustard greens, chopped
1½ teaspoon sugar
450 g (1 lb) frozen broad beans, parboiled and shells removed
3 spring onions, finely chopped
pinch of salt
pinch of white pepper

Preparation time: 15 minutes
Cooking time: 5 minutes

This tasty vegetable dish, which is equally good served hot or cold, comes from the Shanghai region of China.
1. Heat 1 tablespoon of the oil in a wok or frying pan. Drop in the pickles and stir-fry for about 1 minute. Sprinkle on 1 teaspoon of the sugar and then transfer to a bowl.
2. Wipe the pan clean with absorbent kitchen paper and reheat again. Add the remaining oil and stir-fry the broad beans and spring onions with the salt, pepper and remaining sugar.
3. Stir-fry until the colour changes, then return the pickles to the pan, stir well together. Serve on a warm dish.

CLOCKWISE FROM TOP, Stir-fried asparagus; Stir-fried French beans with Chinese dried shrimps and fried mushrooms; Stir-fried broad beans

TIANJIN (NORTH CHINA) SALAD

SERVES 4–5 people with 1 or 2 other dishes

For the Meat jelly:
225 g (8 oz) neck of lamb
4 slices root ginger, shredded
1 tablespoon light soy sauce
1 piece pork skin, about 5 cm (2 inches) square (optional)
600ml (1 pint) water
1 chicken stock cube
3 teaspoons powdered gelatine

For the Dressing:
3 tablespoons finely chopped ginger
2 tablespoons crushed garlic
4 tablespoons finely chopped spring onion
4 tablespoons light soy sauce
3 tablespoons dark soy sauce
4 tablespoons vinegar
4 tablespoons chicken stock
4 tablespoons salad oil
1 tablespoon sesame oil

500 g (1¼ lb) Tianjin or Bok Choy cabbage
225 g (8 oz) mixed vegetables, including sliced cucumber, chicory, tomato, shredded carrots
225 g (8 oz) asparagus spears and young bamboo shoots, parboiled for 3 minutes and well drained
225 g (8 oz) fruit such as melon, pears, mango, kiwi fruit, cut into julienne strips

Preparation time: 35 minutes, plus chilling and setting
Cooking time: 40 minutes

Chinese salads are arranged in a double-decker fashion: a selection of salad vegetables is topped with a layer of fruit. Chinese salad dressing normally consists of finely chopped ginger, garlic and spring onion, blended with a mixture of soy sauce, vinegar, salad oil and a little sesame oil. Other ingredients, such as shrimp sauce, oyster sauce and chopped spiced pickles, are sometimes added to give greater regional definition. In addition, following the traditional Chinese practice of combining vegetables with meat, a small bowl of meat jelly is placed in the centre of the salad: this is chopped up and tossed in with the dressing. For a decorative touch, an edible flower or two may be placed on top of the meat jelly when the salad is brought to the table.

1. First prepare the meat jelly. Chop the lamb into 12 pieces. Add them with the ginger, soy sauce and pork skin, if used, to the water in a saucepan. Bring to the boil, then simmer gently for 30 minutes.
2. Remove the pork skin and lamb bones,

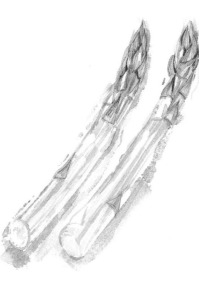

then add the stock cube and gelatine and stir until dissolved. Pour the contents into a medium rice bowl. Allow to cool, then chill in the refrigerator until set (2–3 hours).
3. Meanwhile, prepare the dressing by mixing all the ingredients together in a jug.
4. Arrange all the vegetables evenly on a large dish, and top them with a well-spaced layer of fruit, leaving a hole at the centre of the dish. Turn the meat jelly out into the hole and arrange one or two edible flowers such as nasturtiums, roses, violets, elder flowers or marigolds in the jelly. Just before serving pour the dressing evenly over the salad, chop up the jelly meat and toss well together at the table.

CHICKEN STOCK
Chicken stock, based on the 'throwaway' pieces of a chicken carcase, such as neck, legs, claws and bones, simmered in water with one or two vegetables for flavouring, is widely used in Oriental cookery. It can be the basis of light, refreshing soups, enliven poultry dishes and vegetable stir-fries and enhance dressings, as here.

When buying chicken stock cubes for adding to soups and other dishes, choose varieties which do not contain monosodium glutamate.

YANGTZE (EAST CHINA) SALAD

SERVES 4–5 with 1 or 2 other dishes

For the Chicken and crabmeat jelly:
100 g (4 oz) chicken breast, shredded
100 g (4 oz) crabmeat
350ml (12 fl oz) water
4 slices root ginger, shredded
1 tablespoon light soy sauce
piece pork skin about 5 cm (2 inches) square
  (optional)
1 chicken stock cube
3 teaspoons powdered gelatine

For the Dressing:
3 tablespoons finely chopped root ginger
2 tablespoons crushed garlic
4 tablespoons finely chopped spring onion
3 tablespoons light soy sauce
2 tablespoons dark soy sauce
2 tablespoons dry sherry
4 tablespoons vinegar
4 tablespoons salad oil
1 tablespoon sesame oil

500 g (1¼ lb) Chinese cabbage
225 g (8 oz) mixed vegetables such as celery,
  lettuce, shredded beetroots, bean sprouts,
  shredded turnip
225 g (8 oz) mixed broccoli florets and young
  bamboo shoots, parboiled for 3 minutes
  and well drained
225 g (8 oz) mixed fruits such as grapefruit
  and tangerine segments, melon, grapes,
  apples

Preparation time: 25 minutes, plus
chilling and setting
Cooking time: 20 minutes

1. To prepare the chicken and crabmeat jelly cut the chicken meat into thin strips about 7.5 × 2.5 cm (3 × 1 inch). Break the crabmeat up with a fork. Add to the water in a saucepan, together with the ginger, soy sauce and pork skin if used. Bring to the boil, then simmer gently for 20 minutes. Remove the pork skin if used, add the crumbled stock cube and gelatine and stir until dissolved. Pour into a medium rice bowl, allow to cool, then chill in the refrigerator until set (which should take about 2–3 hours).
2. Meanwhile, prepare the dressing by mixing all the ingredients together in a jug.
3. Arrange the vegetables evenly on a very large serving dish or a small attractive tray, and top them with a well-spaced layer of fruit, leaving a hole in the centre. Turn out the chicken and crabmeat jelly into the hole and arrange one or two edible flowers such as marigold, nasturtium or rose, in the jelly.
4. Just before serving pour the dressing evenly over the salad. Chop up the jelly and toss together at the table.

SESAME
This small seed has a multiplicity of uses in Oriental cookery. The whole seed, raw or roasted, has a sweet, nutty flavour and is used in sweetmeats and as a topping for salads and snacks. Sesame oil is used as a flavouring rather than a cooking medium. A few drops added to the cooking oil used for deep-frying gives a delicious fragrance to such foods as prawns and seafood in batter.

Sesame paste, derived from the seeds, is similar to peanut butter, and has a very rich and aromatic flavour.

PEARL RIVER (SOUTH CHINA) SALAD

SERVES 4–5 with 1 or 2 other dishes

For the Chicken and seafood jelly:
100 g (4 oz) chicken breast, shredded
3 tablespoons fresh prawns
3 tablespoons cooked shelled mussels
3 tablespoons cooked scallops
4 slices root ginger
1 piece pork skin about 2.5 cm (1 inch) square
3 teaspoons light soy sauce
600ml (1 pint) water
1 chicken stock cube
3 teaspoons powdered gelatine
1 tablespoon finely chopped parsley

For Dressing:
3 tablespoons finely chopped root ginger
2 tablespoons crushed peeled garlic
4 tablespoons finely chopped spring onion
3 tablespoons light soy sauce
2 tablespoons dark soy sauce
2 tablespoons dry sherry
4 tablespoons vinegar
4 tablespoons salad oil
1 tablespoon sesame oil

600 g (1¼ lb) Chinese cabbage
225 g (8 oz) mixed vegetables such as celery,
beetroot, red pepper, water chestnuts,
watercress, bean sprouts
225 g (8 oz) mixed cauliflower florets, young
bamboo shoots, young carrots
225 g (8 oz) mixed fruit such as lychees, sliced
kiwi fruit, mangos, orange segments,
pineapple chunks

Preparation time: 25 minutes, plus
chilling and setting
Cooking time: 30 minutes

1. To prepare the chicken and seafood jelly, put the chicken, prawns, mussels, scallops, ginger, pork skin and soy sauce into a saucepan with the water. Bring to the boil, then simmer gently for 25 minutes. Remove the pork skin, add the crumbled stock cube and gelatine and stir until dissolved. Pour into a medium rice bowl, allow to cool, then sprinkle with the parsley and chill in the refrigerator until set (which should take about 2–3 hours).
2. Meanwhile, prepare the dressing by mixing all the ingredients together in a jug.
3. Arrange all the vegetables evenly on a large serving dish or an attractive small tray, and top them with a well-spaced layer of fruit, leaving a hole in the centre. Turn out the chicken and seafood jelly into the hole and arrange one or two edible flowers, such as nasturtium, marigold, or rose in the jelly.
4. Just before serving, stir the dressing and pour it evenly over the salad. Chop up the jelly and toss together at the table.

WATER CHESTNUTS
The Chinese water chestnut (called pi tsi) is a tuber
widely cultivated in China, Japan and the East
Indies. The plant's leaves, not used in cooking,
float on the surface of the water, and the fruit,
or tuber, grows beneath the surface.

The water chestnut is peeled and then sliced or
chopped for cooking and gives a mild, sweet
taste and pleasantly crunchy texture to food.
In this country it is generally sold in
cans, peeled ready for use.

SPICY OKRA

275 g (10 oz) okra, stalks removed and sliced
3 tablespoons vegetable oil
4 shallots, peeled and sliced
1 teaspoon chilli powder
1 teaspoon light soy sauce
1 teaspoon sugar
1 tablespoon lemon juice
250 ml (9 fl oz) water
100 g (4 oz) cooked shrimps

Preparation time: 10 minutes plus blanching
Cooking time: 15 minutes

This exotic vegetable is becoming more and more available not only in ethnic stores but in supermarkets as well. Cooked properly, it has a delicious crunch and lots of flavour, especially with a few spices and cooked shrimps added. Good okra should be pale green and firm with a slight fuzz to the skin. Remove only the hard stalk.

1. Blanch the okra in plenty of boiling water for 2 minutes. This helps to rid the okra of most of its slime. Drain the okra and run it under a cold tap for half a minute or so to retain it's colour.
2. Heat the oil in a wok or frying pan and fry the shallots till soft. Add the okra and cook, stirring all the time, over a high heat for 2 minutes.
3. Add the chilli powder, soy sauce, sugar and lemon juice and stir for 2 minutes. Add the water and cook over a high heat, stirring all the time, for 3 or 4 minutes until almost dry.
4. Add the cooked shrimps, cook for another minute, stirring gently, and serve immediately.

STUFFED COURGETTES

200 g (7 oz) white fish meat
1 teaspoon salt
1 teaspoon cornflour
½ teaspoon pepper
1 tablespoon sesame oil
4 large courgettes
500 ml (18 fl oz) water or fish stock
1 tablespoon oyster sauce
1–2 tablespoons Chinese wine or sherry

Preparation time: 20 minutes
Cooking time: 15 minutes

Any kind of firm vegetable marrow is ideal for this recipe. Large courgettes are especially nice, since they allow you to serve the equivalent of one whole courgette per person. The richness of this dish comes from the fish meat and seasonings in it. Use cod, skate or any large fish. Poach the fish bones for 10 minutes in sufficient water to cover generously to make stock.

1. Fillet the fish, if necessary, place it in a large bowl and knead well with the salt and cornflour. This is to give the fish a smooth, pliable texture. Add the pepper and sesame oil and mix well.
2. Wipe the courgettes, dry them and cut each into rings diagonally. This prevents the stuffing from slipping out. (If using marrows, peel them before cutting into rings.)
3. Stuff each courgette ring with fish meat, patting it in firmly and levelling off with a knife.
4. Bring the stock or water to the boil in a frying pan. Add the oyster sauce. Place the stuffed courgettes, in one layer if possible (no more than two) in the pan, cover and simmer gently for 10 minutes. Turn once. A tablespoon or two of Chinese wine or sherry added in the last few minutes of cooking gives this dish extra bite.

LEFT, Spicy okra; RIGHT, Stuffed courgettes

MIXED VEGETABLE CURRY

3 cabbage leaves
2 carrots
1 medium swede
1 medium aubergine
3 dried chillies, soaked till soft (seeded for
    milder flavour)
½ large onion, peeled and quartered
½ teaspoon turmeric powder
1 tablespoon dried shrimp, soaked till soft
4 candlenuts
1 stalk lemon grass (5 cm/2 inch of thick end)
1 teaspoon shrimp paste
4 tablespoons vegetable oil
300 ml (½ pint) coconut milk
300 ml (½ pint) water
1 tablespoon light soy sauce
1 teaspoon sugar
salt and pepper

Preparation time: 20 minutes
Cooking time: 10 minutes

A rijstaffel classic, i.e. influenced by the Dutch 'rice table' cuisine, this recipe makes use of 'boring' vegetables like cabbage and carrots in an interesting way. Use your imagination and throw in whatever your vegetable garden has to offer, especially turnips, swedes and radishes.

1. Cut the vegetables into even-sized pieces, the actual size being unimportant as long as they are roughly the same.
2. Grind together in a mortar or blender the chillies, onion, turmeric, dried shrimp, candlenuts, lemon grass and shrimp paste.
3. Heat the oil in a frying pan and fry the ground spices for 5 minutes over moderate heat. Add the coconut milk, water and vegetables and cook for 8 minutes. Add the soy sauce and sugar. Add salt and pepper to taste. Serve hot with plain rice and other meat dishes.

AUBERGINE STARTERS

1 large aubergine
1 teaspoon black pepper
2 tablespoons light soy sauce
1 teaspoon sugar
8 tablespoons vegetable oil

Dried shrimp sauce:
2 tablespoons dried shrimps
2 garlic cloves, peeled
1 teaspoon chilli powder
1 teaspoon sugar
1 tablespoon lemon juice

Preparation time: 20 minutes plus marinating
Cooking time: 10 minutes

LEFT, Mixed vegetable curry; RIGHT, Aubergine starters

The large purple aubergines found here are virtually unknown in the East, the equivalent being 'brinjals' which are slimmer and pale green in colour. These are occasionally available at specialist stores, are more succulent and less cotton-woolly. Thai cooks especially love brinjals grown in all shapes and sizes from tiny pea-shaped ones to yard-long monsters. They could be used instead of the aubergine in this recipe.

1. Remove the stalk from the aubergine. Cut into two lengthwise and again into half-moon shapes, each 1 cm (½ inch) thick. With a sharp knife, score cross cuts on both surfaces of the aubergine slices, making sure you do not cut through them.
2. Mix the pepper, soy sauce and sugar together and marinate the aubergine in the mixture for a few minutes.
3. Meanwhile, make the dried shrimp sauce. Soak the dried shrimp in hot water until soft. Drain, then pound in a mortar or blender with the garlic until fine. Add the remaining ingredients and stir well.
4. Heat the oil in a wok or frying pan and fry the aubergines a few slices at a time for 2 or 3 minutes until the surface is slightly crisp and the skin changes colour.
5. Serve with the dried shrimp sauce spread over.

SPICY LONG BEANS WITH FISH CAKE

8 long or runner beans
1 block fish cake
3 tablespoons vegetable oil
2 garlic cloves, peeled and crushed
1 tablespoon chilli bean paste
150 ml (¼ pint) water
1 teaspoon salt

Preparation time: 10 minutes
Cooking time: 10 minutes

A very symbolic vegetable in China – anything long will be eaten by the Chinese for the assurance of longevity they imply – long or runner beans are also readily available. They have a lovely nutty flavour and are very versatile in omelettes, fried rice, curries and raw salads. All Chinese supermarkets in this country sell a range of cooked, chilled or frozen fish cakes in small rectangular blocks.

1. Cut the beans into 5 cm (2 inch) lengths, wash and drain. Slice the fish cake into lengths of roughly the same thickness as the beans.

2. Heat the oil in a wok or frying pan and fry the garlic till light brown. Add the chilli paste and cook the mixture, stirring all the time, for a minute.

3. Add the long beans, cook, stirring well for 2–3 minutes then add the fish cake and water. Cook over a high heat, stirring well for a minute or two. Add salt to taste and serve immediately on a warmed dish.

FESTIVE VEGETABLE ACHAR

5 cabbage leaves
1 cucumber
3 carrots, trimmed
1 head cauliflower
1.5 litres (2½ pints) vinegar
20 shallots, peeled and chopped
2 tablespoons shredded ginger
1 thumb-size piece fresh turmeric
3 red chillies
2 teaspoons shrimp paste
5 candlenuts
1 large onion, peeled and chopped
6 tablespoons vegetable oil
200 g (7 oz) ground nuts
3 tablespoons sugar
4 tablespoons sesame seeds

Preparation time: 45 minutes
Cooking time: 8 minutes

This spicy pickle came to South-East Asia with merchants from North India some centuries ago and was adopted and adapted with great relish by the migrant people who had already evolved a spicy cuisine from the best of Chinese, Malay and Indonesian cooking. It is prepared in great vats for serving during Chinese New Year.

1. Cut the cabbage into about 5 × 1 cm (2 × ½ inch) strips. Remove the pith from the cucumber and cut into similar-size pieces. Cut the carrots likewise. Separate the cauliflower into small florets.

2. Bring the vinegar to the boil and scald the cabbage, cucumber, carrots, cauliflower and shallots, a handful at a time, for a minute. Drain well.

3. Grind together in a mortar or blender the ginger, turmeric, chillies, shrimp paste, candlenuts and onion.

4. Heat the oil in a wok or frying pan and fry the ground spices for 5 minutes. Place in a glass or enamel (not metal) bowl and mix in the vegetables thoroughly.

5. Refrigerate for at least one day, preferably several. To serve, mix in the ground nuts and sugar and sprinkle the sesame seeds over the top.

LEFT, Festive vegetable achar; RIGHT, Spicy long beans with fish cake

ONION AND HAM OMELETTE

SERVES 2

4 tablespoons vegetable oil
½ large onion, peeled and chopped
1 red pepper, seeded and diced
4 eggs, beaten
½ tablespoon salt
½ teaspoon pepper
3 tablespoons cubed ham
red pepper rings, to garnish

Preparation time: 10 minutes
Cooking time: 8 minutes

Obviously derived from the cooking of Europe, this recipe may be of Dutch origin, as the first Western-style tinned meat to reach the East some five decades ago was Dutch ham and the ubiquitous Spam. Or perhaps a Welsh English literature teacher liked his rarebit for tiffin! Which probably explains this omelette better. Tinned ham was and still is popular as a fried rice ingredient in South-East Asia but is rarely eaten on its own.

1. Heat the oil in a wok or frying pan and fry the onion till light brown. Add the red pepper and cook, stirring, for a minute.
2. Pour in the eggs, add the salt and pepper and swirl the pan around. Add the cubed ham, spreading it evenly over the egg mixture and cook the omelette over a moderate heat until the bottom side has set.
3. Cut into four and flip each piece over to brown. Cook for another 2–3 minutes till crisp around the edges.
4. Cut up further and serve hot. Serve garnished with red pepper rings and with a chilli or tomato sauce dip.

TROPICAL GREAT SALAD

1 head cos lettuce
1 head chicory
1 cucumber
1 pineapple
1 star fruit (carambola)

Sauce:
3 red chillies
2 tablespoons dried shrimps, soaked till soft
4 garlic cloves, peeled
2 tablespoons lime juice
1 tablespoon sugar
1 tablespoon fish sauce
2 tablespoons finely chopped nuts
1 tablespoon chopped spring onion

Preparation time: 20 minutes, plus chilling

This is in the best tradition of South-East Asian salads, with a sauce that is a complex blend of ingredients. Traditionally as many as ten different vegetables and fruits are used, ranging from tapioca leaves to raw papaya, banana buds, sweet basil, lime leaves and fresh coriander. Whatever fruits are in season are added to the bowl. A combination of salad greens like cos, chicory and cucumber make an interesting variation. Add green mango, pineapple and star fruit for something 'different'.

1. Wash and dry the cos and chicory and separate into individual leaves. Slice the cucumber lengthwise twice and remove the central seeds. Slice into long crudités.
2. Skin the pineapple, remove the hard core and cut into half-moon pieces. Remove the rind from each segment of star fruit and cut into 1 cm (½ inch) star shapes. Remove the seeds with the tip of a sharp knife. Chill the salad.
3. For the sauce, grind together the red chillies, shrimps and garlic cloves then mix together with the remaining ingredients.
4. Serve the salad and sauce separately.

LEFT, Tropical great salad, with chilli and shrimp sauce; RIGHT, Onion and ham omelette

# MEAT

Perhaps because it has always been scarce in the Far East, meat is treated very creatively in Oriental cookery. To prove the point, recipes here range from simple but splendidly tasty stir-fries of beef, lamb and pork to an unusual steamed pudding based on pork and cauliflower.

Stir-fried beef and pineapple (see page 43)

HOT SPICED CHINESE PEPPERED STEAK

SERVES 4–5 with 1 or 2 other dishes

1kg (2 lb) rump steak
¾ teaspoon salt
½ teaspoon freshly ground black pepper
1 chilli pepper, seeded, shredded and very finely chopped or minced
2 tablespoons dark soy sauce
1 tablespoon hoisin sauce
1 medium red pepper, seeded
1 medium green pepper, seeded
4 tablespoons vegetable oil
2 tablespoons dry sherry
3 slices root ginger, shredded and very finely chopped or minced

Preparation time: 10 minutes, plus marinating
Cooking time: 6 minutes

This is the Chinese version of the Western cuisine's 'pepper steak', in which the beef is cut into small pieces that are more easily managed with chopsticks. Soy and hoisin sauces add to the Chinese flavour.

1. Cut the steak along the grain into three equal pieces. Sprinkle with the salt, pepper, chilli pepper, soy sauce and hoisin sauce. Leave to marinate for 30 minutes. Cut the sweet peppers into thin strips about 7.5 × 1 cm (3 × ½ inch).

2. Heat the oil in a wok or frying pan. When hot lay the three pieces of beef side by side in the sizzling oil in the pan. Shake and fry over high heat for 2 minutes. Turn the beef and cook for 1½ minutes over high heat on the other side. Remove the pieces of beef from the pan and set aside on a hot dish.

3. Add the sweet pepper strips to the wok or pan. Stir-fry for 30 seconds, then add the sherry and ginger and stir-fry for a further 30 seconds.

4. Spread out the pepper mixture on a hot serving dish. Cut each piece of beef into four and arrange on top of the bed of peppers and serve.

QUICK-FRIED BEEF RIBBONS WITH GINGER, CARROTS AND SPRING ONIONS

SERVES 4–5 with 1 or 2 other dishes

600 g (1¼ lb) lean beef (rump, fillet or topside)
2 tablespoons dark soy sauce
2 tablespoons hoisin sauce
¾ teaspoon sugar
1 tablespoon dry sherry
pinch pepper
2 spring onions, trimmed and chopped
4 tablespoons vegetable oil
3 slices root ginger, shredded
1 young (or finger) carrot, shredded

Preparation time: 15 minutes, plus marinating
Cooking time: 5 minutes

Use good quality beef for this dish so that quick cooking is possible. Its great flavour makes it a universal favourite both at home and at Chinese restaurants.

1. Using a very sharp knife, cut the beef into thin slices, then into double match-stick-size ribbons. Place the beef in a large bowl. Add half the soy and hoisin sauces, the sugar, sherry and pepper, stir together well and leave the beef to marinate in the mixture for 15 minutes.

2. Cut the spring onions diagonally into 5 cm (2 inch) pieces.

3. Heat the oil in a wok or frying pan. When hot add the shredded ginger and carrots, spread them out evenly over the pan and stir-fry over a high heat for 1 minute. Add the marinated beef and stir-fry briskly with the ginger and carrots, for 1½ minutes.

4. Add the remaining sauces, with any remaining marinade. Continue to stir-fry briskly for a further 30 seconds still over a high heat. Sprinkle over the spring onion, stir and turn once more and serve immediately.

Variation: For a hotter dish, add 2 green chilli peppers and 1 dried red chilli pepper to the ingredients, removing the stems and seeds; add the chilli peppers to the pan with the shredded ginger and carrots before the beef is added. This variation on the basic recipe comes from the Upper Yangtze.

LEFT, Quick-fried beef ribbons with ginger, carrots and spring onions; RIGHT, Hot spiced Chinese peppered steak

STIR-FRIED BEEF RIBBON NOODLES IN OYSTER SAUCE

SERVES 4–5 with 1 or 2 other dishes
700 g (1½ lb) lean beef (rump, fillet or
    topside)
1 teaspoon salt
2 tablespoons light soy sauce
2½ tablespoons oyster sauce
5 tablespoons vegetable oil
2 celery sticks
100 g (4 oz) mangetout
2 spring onions, trimmed
1 young (or finger) carrot
350 g (12 oz) Chinese noodles or spaghetti
3 slices root ginger, shredded
2 tablespoons butter
2 tablespoons dry sherry

Preparation time: 20 minutes, plus
marinating
Cooking time: 15 minutes

An exceptionally tasty and satisfying version of stir-fried beef, this recipe calls for two sauces – oyster and soy – to be added to the beef.

1. Using a sharp knife, cut the beef into thin slices, then into double matchstick-size ribbons. Sprinkle with half the salt, soy sauce, and oyster sauce and 1 tablespoon of the oil. Stir well, then leave to marinate for 30 minutes.
2. Clean the celery and cut into double matchstick strips. Top and tail the mangetout and cut into similar strips. Cut the spring onions diagonally into 5 cm (2 inch) lengths. Cut the carrot into matchstick strips.
3. Parboil the noodles for 5–6 minutes (or spaghetti for 10 minutes), take off the heat and leave to stand in the hot water for a further 5 minutes. Drain.

4. Heat the remaining oil in a deep-sided frying pan, wok or large saucepan. When hot, add the ginger and all the shredded vegetables. Stir-fry over high heat for 1½ minutes. Add the beef with the marinade and stir-fry with the vegetables for 2 minutes. Remove half the contents of the pan and set aside.
5. Add the noodles to the pan and briefly stir-fry with the vegetables and beef. Reduce the heat to low, add the butter and sprinkle with the remaining sauces. Stir-fry for a further 2½ minutes.
6. Transfer the contents of the pan to a large, deep-sided hot serving dish. Place the reserved beef, sauce and vegetables in a clean pan. Pour sherry over them and bring quickly to the boil. Pour the mixture over the noodles, beef and vegetables and serve immediately.

SLICED MARINATED BEEF WITH SCRAMBLED EGGS

750 g (1½ lb) lean beef (rump, fillet or
    topside)
1 teaspoon finely chopped ginger
1 teaspoon salt
1 teaspoon sugar
¼ teaspoon freshly ground black pepper
1 teaspoon light soy sauce
1 teaspoon hoisin sauce
1 tablespoon vegetable oil
1 tablespoon Chinese rice wine or dry sherry
6 eggs
about 200 ml (7 fl oz) vegetable oil
4 spring onions, chopped

Preparation time: 20 minutes, plus
marinating
Cooking time: 4–5 minutes

This is one of the great repertoire of Chinese dishes created to accompany rice. Seasoned beef, quickly stir-fried, and lightly cooked eggs amply sprinkled with spring onions give it a unique appeal.

1. Using a very sharp knife, cut the beef into thin slices, then into 5 × 3 cm (2 × 1½ inch) pieces. Place the beef in a bowl and add the ginger, half the salt, sugar, pepper, soy sauce, hoisin sauce, oil and Chinese wine or sherry. Stir well, then marinate for 1 hour, turning once every 15 minutes.
2. Beat the eggs with the remaining salt for 30 seconds.
3. Heat a wok or frying-pan over a high heat for 15 seconds. Pour in 150 ml

(¼ pint) of the oil and heat for 30 seconds. Add the beef and stir-fry over a high heat for 1¼ minutes. Remove the beef and drain away the oil. Mix the well-drained beef with the beaten eggs.
4. Heat the remaining oil in a clean wok or frying-pan. When hot add half the spring onion and stir-fry for 10 seconds over a medium heat then pour in the egg and beef mixture and stir-fry gently over a medium heat for 1½ minutes or until the eggs have set.
5. Serve on a hot serving dish, sprinkled with the remaining spring onion.

*LEFT, Stir-fried beef ribbon noodles in oyster sauce;
RIGHT, Sliced marinated beef with scrambled eggs*

STIR-FRIED BEEF AND PINEAPPLE

200 g (7 oz) sirloin
2 tablespoons sherry
1 tablespoon soy sauce
1 teaspoon cornflour
4 tablespoons vegetable oil
2 garlic cloves, peeled and crushed
½ red pepper, seeded and diced
10 pineapple cubes
5 tablespoons pineapple juice
3 tablespoons water
1 teaspoon salt

Preparation time: 15 minutes, plus marinating
Cooking time: 8 minutes

Pineapples pop up in many South-East Asian dishes of Chinese origin for two reasons. They are cheap and plentiful and have a curious chameleon quality that marries well with meats, poultry and seafood. Their tartness also cuts down on fat and their natural sweetness rounds off the flavour of a sauce, much as a pinch of sugar does. For a spicier dish, you could replace the red pepper with seeded and sliced red chillies.

1. Cut the sirloin into thin slices 5 × 2.5 × 1 cm (2 × 1 × ½ inch) thick. Beat slightly with a meat mallet.
2. Marinate the sirloin pieces in the sherry, soy sauce and cornflour for 10 minutes.
3. Heat the oil in a wok or frying pan and fry the garlic till light brown. Add the red pepper and stir for ½ minute over a high heat.
4. Drain the beef and add to the pan, together with the pineapple. Stir for 2 minutes and add any remaining marinade mixed with the pineapple juice, water and salt. Stir for 1 minute and serve hot.

CINNAMON BEEF

750 g (1½ lb) sirloin
5 tablespoons vegetable oil
4 garlic cloves, peeled and sliced
1 large onion, peeled and sliced
2 sticks cinnamon, each 5 cm (2 inch) long
5 cloves
2 tablespoons dark soy sauce
2 tablespoons oyster sauce
1 litre (1¾ pints) water
2 teaspoons salt
½ teaspoon pepper
spring onions, to garnish

Preparation time: 10 minutes
Cooking time: 1 hour 10 minutes

This is believed to have derived from a Portuguese pot roast recipe brought to South-East Asia some three centuries ago. That intrepid traveller Vasco Da Gama came upon the town of Malacca on the west coast of Malaya and established an enclave early in the 16th century. The Eurasian community that resulted from ensuing mixed marriages between Portugese, Indian and Chinese still exists today, its cuisine a curious but none-the-less delicious blend of European and Oriental styles.

1. Cut the beef into three pieces against the grain. Heat the oil in a frying pan and brown the beef all over.
2. Remove the beef from the pan, add the garlic and onion and fry till light brown. Transfer to a deep pot, add the beef and all remaining ingredients.
3. Simmer on a moderate heat for 20 minutes and on a low heat for 40 minutes, checking the liquid level and topping up with water if necessary. Taste and adjust seasoning towards the end of cooking time, if necessary.
4. When cooked, the sauce should be quite concentrated. To serve, slice the beef thinly and pour the sauce over. Garnish the dish with spring onions.

LEFT, Stir-fried beef and pineapple; RIGHT, Cinnamon beef

QUICK-FRIED SLICED GARLIC LAMB WITH YOUNG LEEKS

SERVES 4–6 with 1 or 2 other dishes
450 g (1 lb) leg of lamb, boned
1½ teaspoons salt
¼ teaspoon freshly ground black pepper
3 garlic cloves, peeled and crushed
1 tablespoon dark soy sauce
1 tablespoon hoisin sauce
1 tablespoon dry sherry
5½ tablespoons vegetable oil
225 g (8 oz) young leeks
1 tablespoon light soy sauce
2 tablespoons chicken stock

Preparation time: 20 minutes, plus marinating
Cooking time: 3 minutes

This dish, positively reeking of garlic, is widely popular with the working people of Beijing (Peking) and North China.
1. Using a very sharp knife, cut the lamb into thin slices, then into double matchstick-size ribbons. Place the lamb in a bowl. Add the salt, the pepper, half the garlic, the dark soy and hoisin sauces, the sherry and 1 tablespoon of the oil. Mix well, then leave to marinate for 30 minutes.
2. Clean the leeks thoroughly, trim and cut diagonally into 5 cm (2 inch) pieces.
3. Heat the remaining oil in a wok or frying pan until very hot. Add the lamb with the remaining marinade. Spread evenly over the pan and stir-fry quickly over a high heat for no more than 20 seconds. Remove and set aside.

4. Add the leeks and remaining salt to the pan and stir-fry quickly for 1 minute. Add the light soy sauce and stock and stir-fry quickly for a further 30 seconds. Add the lamb and the remaining garlic and stir-fry with the leeks over a high heat for a further 4 seconds. Serve immediately.

MINCED LAMB SAVOURY

4 tablespoons ghee
½ onion, peeled and sliced
1 teaspoon chilli powder
1 tablespoon coriander powder
9 tablespoons water
1 tomato, chopped
1 small bunch mint, chopped
pinch of nutmeg
400 g (14 oz) minced lamb
2 teaspoons salt
fresh coriander leaves, to garnish

Preparation time: 10 minutes
Cooking time: about 15 minutes

1. Heat the ghee in a heavy-bottomed frying pan until it bubbles. Fry the onion until soft.
2. Mix the chilli and coriander with 5 tablespoons of the water and add to the pan. Fry for 1 minute, then add the tomato, mint, nutmeg and minced lamb. Stir for 2 minutes and add the salt and the remaining water. Bring the heat up to high and continue cooking, stirring, for another 5 minutes.
3. Serve garnished with sprigs of fresh coriander. Any leftover makes a delicious sandwich filling, topped with slices of cucumber.

FROM THE TOP, Quick-fried sliced garlic lamb with young leeks; Minced lamb savoury

CHINESE/MOSLEM LONG-SIMMERED GINGER LAMB

SERVES 4–6 with 1 or 2 other dishes
1 kg (2¼ lb) leg of lamb, boned
6 slices root ginger
2 teaspoons salt
2 onions, peeled and thinly sliced
5 tablespoons dry sherry or Chinese rice wine
2 tablespoons chopped coriander

Dip one:
4 tablespoons finely chopped spring onion
3 garlic cloves, peeled and finely chopped
5 tablespoons dark soy sauce
3 tablespoons dry sherry
2 tablespoons chicken stock
3 tablespoons vegetable oil
2 teaspoons sesame oil

Dip Two:
5 slices root ginger, finely chopped
2 tablespoons wine vinegar
2 tablespoons dry sherry or Chinese rice wine
1 tablespoon vegetable oil
1 teaspoon sesame oil

Dip Three:
5 tablespoons peanut butter
2 tablespoons sesame oil
2 tablespoons vegetable oil
3 tablespoons chicken stock
1 tablespoon chilli sauce
1 tablespoon dry sherry

Preparation time: 25 minutes
Cooking time: 1 hour 40 minutes
Oven: 180°C, 350°F, Gas Mark 4

This is a simply cooked dish, made extra delectable by the dip sauces which are served with the lamb.

1. Using a very sharp knife, cut the lamb into thin slices, then into 7.5 × 4 cm (3 × 1½ inch) pieces.
2. Place the ginger slices at the bottom of a flameproof casserole. Cover them with the lamb slices. Sprinkle with salt and cover with the onion. Pour in water to cover and add the sherry or Chinese wine.
3. Bring slowly to the boil and boil gently for 5 minutes. Cover the casserole, and cook in a preheated oven for 1½ hours. Check from time to time to make sure the casserole is not drying out and add water or stock if necessary.
4. Meanwhile, thoroughly mix together the ingredients for the dipping sauces in three separate bowls, placed on the table for the diners to help themselves. Sprinkle the lamb casserole with coriander and serve with the dipping sauces.

CHINESE RICE WINE
Rice wine is the most popular alcoholic beverage of China and is commonly called 'yellow wine' on account of its golden colour. The best yellow wine is said to come from Shaoshing, in Chekiang province. It is readily available in specialist Chinese food stores in this country. Since it is very similar, both in colour and flavour, to dry sherry, the latter makes a good substitute for it.

DOUBLE-COOKED LAMB

SERVES 4–5 with 1 or 2 other dishes
700 g (1½ lb) leg of lamb, boned
¾ teaspoon salt
2 slices root ginger, shredded and finely
    chopped
2 tomatoes
2 onions, peeled and sliced
1 tablespoon yellow bean sauce
1 tablespoon light soy sauce
1 tablespoon chilli sauce
2 tablespoons tomato purée
3 garlic cloves, peeled and crushed
1 teaspoon sugar
1 tablespoon dry sherry
2 tablespoons chicken stock

Preparation time: 25 minutes
Cooking time: 45 minutes

This is an Upper Yangtze, Szechuan recipe for lamb, with the same appeal as the better known Szechuan dish, double-cooked pork.

1. Cook the lamb in a large saucepan of boiling water for 35 minutes. Drain and allow to cool. Cut the lamb into 1 cm (½ inch) thick slices, then again into 5 × 2.5 cm (2 × 1 inch) pieces. Rub them with the salt and ginger. Slice the tomatoes thinly.
2. Heat the oil in a wok or frying pan. Add the onion and tomatoes and stir-fry over medium heat for 3 minutes. Add all the remaining ingredients and stir-fry for 1 minute. Reduce the heat to low and simmer gently for a further 2 minutes.
3. Add the sliced lamb and turn gently in the sauce over a high heat for a further 2 minutes. Serve immediately.

YOGURT LAMB CHOPS

8 lamb chops on the bone
150 g (5 oz) plain, unsweetened yogurt
1 tablespoon lemon juice
2 teaspoons salt
1 teaspoon ground black pepper
1 teaspoon turmeric powder
1 tablespoon chopped ginger
pinch of nutmeg
400 ml (14 fl oz) oil for deep-frying
1 tablespoon chopped mint

Preparation time: 10 minutes, plus
marinating
Cooking time: about 20 minutes

South-East Asian cooking reflects much Indian influence but mainly from the sub-continent's southern provinces as most migrants came from there. As the colonies prospered, wealthy textile merchants and jewellery craftsmen came from North India to settle in Singapore, Malaysia and Hong Kong in the early 20th century. With the Moglai-style cooking they also brought with them a passion for yogurt. Interestingly, their 12th-century ancestors, the wild, nomadic Mongols also influenced Northern Chinese cooking.

1. Trim off any gristle from the lamb. Combine all the ingredients except the oil and mint and marinate the chops for half an hour, turning once in the marinade. Remove each chop from the marinade by holding the bone end and shaking off any excess. Reserve the marinade.
2. Heat the oil to 180°C/350°F or until a cube of bread browns in 30 seconds and deep-fry a few chops at a time till crisp. This should take about 3–4 minutes, depending on the thickness of your chop.
3. Add the chopped mint to the marinade, turn into a saucepan and simmer over low heat for 2 minutes. Cool and serve as a dip for the lamb chops.

LEFT, Double-cooked lamb; RIGHT, Yogurt lamb chops

SPARE RIBS IN CAPITAL SAUCE

SERVES 4–5 with 1 or 2 other dishes
900 g (2 lb) meaty spare ribs
450 ml (¾ pint) chicken stock
5 slices root ginger
2 tablespoons yellow bean sauce
2 tablespoons dark soy sauce
2 tablespoons hoisin sauce
1 chicken stock cube
2 tablespoons sugar
pinch of freshly ground black pepper
1 tablespoon clear honey
spring onion, to garnish

Preparation time: 10 minutes
Cooking time: 35 minutes

The Capital Sauce in this recipe for spare ribs is widely used in Beijing (Peking), hence its name. In the recipe, the ribs are cooked in a rapidly reducing stock which becomes, first, a stock, then an extremely tasty glaze on the ribs.

1. Cook the spare ribs in a saucepan of boiling water over a high heat for 15 minutes, then drain well.
2. Place the spare ribs in a large flameproof casserole. Pour in the stock, then add the remaining ingredients. Bring quickly to the boil, uncovered, and cook briskly for 20 minutes, frequently turning the ribs in the sauce to coat evenly. When the sauce is reduced to one quarter, reduce the heat and continue to cook, turning the spare ribs occasionally, until the sauce has become a glaze on them. Turn once more and serve immediately, garnished with spring onion.

SPICY SPARE RIBS

750 g (1½ lb) spare ribs
1 tablespoon hoisin sauce
1 tablespoon oyster sauce
1 tablespoon sugar
3 tablespoons vegetable oil
3 tablespoons Chinese wine or sherry
2 tablespoons ginger juice
1 teaspoon pepper
½ teaspoon cayenne pepper
200 ml (7 fl oz) water

Preparation time: 10 minutes, plus cooling and marinating
Cooking time: 18 minutes

To think that not so long ago, butchers in this country had to pay for spare ribs to be carted away! Chinese takeaways probably boomed from this strange extravagance. The truth is, spare ribs have always been highly prized in China even when pork is cheap and abundant. There is good reason, as they make excellent stock and the succulent meat can be stripped off and added to fried rice and noodles. When coated with a rich marinade they are best grilled, as deep-frying tends to dry up pork.

1. Ask your butcher to separate the ribs and cut each one into roughly 7.5 cm (3 inch) pieces.
2. Combine all the ingredients except the spare ribs and bring to the boil in a large saucepan.
3. Add the ribs to the pan and simmer for 5 minutes. Take off the heat to cool and allow to marinate for at least half an hour.
4. Remove the ribs from the marinade and cook under a pre-heated grill for 3 or 4 minutes.
5. Meanwhile, reduce the marinade by boiling down over a high heat for 5 minutes. Serve it as a dip for the grilled ribs.

FROM THE TOP, Spare ribs in capital sauce; Spicy spare ribs

SOY-BRAISED PORK WITH CHESTNUTS

SERVES 4–5 with 1 or 2 other dishes
450 g (1 lb) lean loin of pork
450 g (1 lb) belly of pork
350 g (12 oz) chestnuts, peeled
4 slices root ginger
2 tablespoons sugar
3 tablespoons dark soy sauce
1 tablespoon yellow bean sauce
2 tablespoons hoisin sauce
600 ml (1 pint) chicken stock
1 chicken stock cube, crumbled
3 tablespoons dry sherry
chopped spring onion, to garnish

Preparation time: 15 minutes
Cooking time: 1 hour 35 minutes

A rich, hearty dish, ideal for people with big appetites! Use ready-skinned chestnuts, available frozen or in cans, to cut down on the preparation time.

1. Using a very sharp knife, cut the loin and belly of pork into 7.5 × 5 cm (3 × 2 inch) pieces about 2.5 cm (1 inch) thick. Parboil for 10 minutes, then drain and remove the skins. Discard the water in which the meats were boiled.
2. Place the pork pieces and chestnuts in a flameproof casserole. Add all the remaining ingredients except the sherry and bring slowly to the boil, turning to mix well.
3. Reduce the heat to low and simmer gently for 45 minutes, then stir in the sherry. Simmer for a further 30 minutes. If the casserole shows signs of drying out, add water or stock as necessary.
4. Serve straight from the casserole, garnished with spring onion.

STEAMED MINCED PORK PUDDING WITH CAULIFLOWER

SERVES 4–5 with 1 or 2 other dishes
450 g (1 lb) minced pork
2 tablespoons finely chopped Chinese green pickles, 'snow pickle' (pickled leeks), or gherkins
2 tablespoons cornflour
1 egg, beaten
1 teaspoon sugar
pinch of freshly ground black pepper
1½ teaspoons vegetable oil
2 tablespoons light soy sauce
1 medium cauliflower
¾ teaspoon salt
2 tablespoons dry sherry

To garnish:
sprigs fresh parsley
cauliflower florets

Preparation time: 15 minutes
Cooking time: 1 hour 35 minutes

This is very much an easy-to-produce home-cooked dish, useful when a large family is being catered for. It is usually served with rice.

1. Mix the pork with the chopped pickle, cornflour, beaten egg, sugar, black pepper, oil and soy sauce, until thoroughly combined.
2. Remove the cauliflower stem and cut it into six pieces. Break the cauliflower into florets. Pack the cauliflower into the bottom of a large, deep, heatproof basin. Sprinkle evenly with the salt and sherry. Add the minced pork mixture and press down well.
3. Place the basin in a steamer or in a large saucepan with boiling water to come halfway up the sides of the basin. Steam vigorously for about 1 hour 35 minutes, checking the water level occasionally and topping up, if necessary. When the dish is ready, serve straight from the basin at the table, garnished with parsley and cauliflower florets.

LEFT, Soy-braised pork with chestnuts; RIGHT, Steamed minced pork pudding with cauliflower

STIR-FRIED LIVER WITH GINGER WINE

350 g (12 oz) calf's liver
4 tablespoons vegetable oil
½ onion, peeled and sliced
2 tablespoons root ginger, shredded
4 slices ginger
2 tablespoons ginger wine
1 tablespoon oyster sauce
2 tablespoons sesame oil
1 tablespoon dark soy sauce
½ tablespoon pepper
1 teaspoon sugar
150 ml (5 fl oz) water
2 stalks spring onions, cut into 4 cm (1½ inch)
    lengths

Preparation time: 15 minutes
Cooking time: 5 minutes

Liver is not one of the easiest meats to cook but when properly done is delicious. As it toughens very quickly, stir-frying is one of the best ways to treat this offal. Calf's liver, though more expensive than pig's liver, has a better flavour and texture, especially when cooked quickly. The traditional ingredients include ginger juice and Chinese wine, but using ginger wine instead cuts down preparation time and has as much flavour.

1. Cut the liver into thin slices about 5 × 2.5 × 1 cm (2 × 1 × ½ inch).
2. Heat the oil and fry the onion and ginger for 2 minutes over a high heat. Add the liver and cook, stirring, for 30 seconds. Add all the other ingredients, except the spring onions, and cook, stirring well, for another minute. The liver should be just done with no trace of blood. Test by piercing one piece with a fork.
3. In the last minute of cooking time add the spring onions and stir well before serving.

CRISPY PORK IN HOT SWEET AND SOUR SAUCE

750 g (1½ lb) lean loin of pork
¾ teaspoon salt
3 tablespoons cornflour
1 egg white
about 300 ml (½ pint) vegetable oil
For the sauce:
1 tablespoon vegetable oil
4 slices root ginger, shredded
1 green chilli pepper, seeded and shredded
1 dried red chilli pepper, shredded
1 small carrot, shredded
1 medium onion, peeled and finely sliced
2 garlic cloves, peeled and crushed
2 tablespoons light soy sauce
1 tablespoon hoisin sauce
1 tablespoon vinegar
1 tablespoon sugar
1 tablespoon tomato purée
1 tablespoon dry sherry

Preparation time: 10 minutes
Cooking time: 12 minutes

Essentially a 'sweet and sour' pork dish, this is made spicier than usual by the addition of chilli powder into the stir-frying.

1. Cut the pork into 5 × 4 cm (2 × 1½ inch) pieces about 1 cm (½ inch) thick. Sprinkle them with the salt and cornflour, rubbing in well, and brush all over with egg white.
2. Heat the oil in a wok or frying pan. When very hot add the pork pieces and spread evenly over the pan. Stir-fry over a high heat for 1 minute. Reduce the heat to medium/low, and continue to stir-fry for 5–6 minutes. Remove the pork and drain on absorbent kitchen paper.
3. In a clean pan, heat the oil for the sauce and fry the ginger, chilli peppers, shredded carrot and onion for 2 minutes. Add all the remaining ingredients and stir for 15 seconds.
4. Raise the heat to high and add the pork pieces to the sauce. Continue to turn and stir the pork in the bubbling sauce for 30 seconds, then serve.

LEFT, Crispy pork in hot sweet and sour sauce; RIGHT, Stir-fried liver with ginger wine

TIFFIN PORK CHOPS

4 boneless pork chops
1 egg, lightly beaten
1 packet breadcrumbs
300 ml (½ pint) vegetable oil
½ onion, peeled and sliced
2 tomatoes, quartered
1 tablespoon Worcestershire sauce
2 tablespoons tomato sauce
1 tablespoon soy sauce
5 tablespoons water

Preparation time: 15 minutes
Cooking time: 25 minutes

British colonial influence in South-East Asia did not end with pith helmets and gin slings. It also created new words like 'tiffin' instead of lunch and 'Mullagatawnee', originally an Indian curry soup called Mooloogatahnee. It also gave us Worcestershire sauce, chips, peas and the penchant for tapioca pudding – horrors of school meals notwithstanding. This hybrid is popular among Chinese Anglophiles.

1. Beat the pork chops with a meat mallet for a few minutes and cut each chop into four pieces. Coat the pieces with the beaten egg, drain off any excess and toss them thoroughly in breadcrumbs.

2. Heat the oil in a wok or frying pan and fry the pork until golden brown. Drain on absorbent kitchen paper and set aside.

3. Remove all but 3 tablespoons of the oil from the pan and fry the onion till soft. Add the tomatoes, sauces and water and bring to a quick boil.

4. Lower the heat and simmer till well blended and the tomatoes are soft. Add the pork to the sauce and heat through. Serve with bread or rice.

STIR-FRIED SHREDDED HAM WITH BEAN SPROUTS

SERVES 4–5 with 1 or 2 other dishes
250 g (9 oz) sliced cooked ham
3 garlic cloves, peeled
3 slices root ginger
3 spring onions
4 tablespoons vegetable oil
400 g (14 oz) fresh bean sprouts
2 tablespoons light soy sauce
1 tablespoon dry sherry
1 teaspoon sesame oil

Preparation time: 15 minutes
Cooking time: 5 minutes

An easy-to-prepare, quickly cooked dish.

1. Cut the ham into matchstick-size strips. Crush the garlic, shred the ginger and cut the spring onions into 2.5 cm (1 inch) lengths.

2. Heat the oil in a wok or frying pan. When hot add the spring onion, garlic and ginger. Stir-fry over a medium heat for 30 seconds. Add the bean sprouts and ham, raise the heat to high, and stir-fry for 1½ minutes.

3. Sprinkle with the remaining ingredients and stir-fry for a further minute. Serve immediately.

FROM THE TOP, Tiffin pork chops; Stir-fried shredded ham with bean sprouts

POULTRY

If chicken is your preference, you will find much inspiration here, with recipes ranging from whole roast chicken, Chinese-style, to some memorable stir-fries. And there are recipes for duck, quail and goose, too, all adding up to a fine variety of ways to cook poultry.

Coconut-grilled chicken (see page 71)

CHINESE ROAST CHICKEN

SERVES 4–5 with 1 or 2 other dishes
1.5 kg (3½ lb) roasting chicken
1½ teaspoons salt
2 garlic cloves, peeled and crushed
3 slices root ginger, finely chopped
1 tablespoon dark soy sauce
1 tablespoon vegetable oil
¼ teaspoon freshly ground black pepper

Preparation time: 15 minutes, plus drying and marinating
Cooking time: 1 hour 5 minutes
Oven: 200°C, 400°F, Gas Mark 6

A dish to be recommended since it is easy to prepare and straightforward to cook. Rubbing the skin of the bird with soy sauce gives it an additional flavour.
1. Wash and dry the chicken thoroughly inside and out. Place it in an airy spot to dry for 2–3 hours. Rub it inside and out with salt. Combine the remaining ingredients and rub the chicken all over with the mixture. Leave to marinate for 1 hour.
2. Place the chicken on a rack in a roasting pan and roast in a pre-heated oven for 1 hour 5 minutes, basting with the juices from time to time.

QUICK-FRIED SLIVERS OF CHICKEN WITH ASPARAGUS

SERVES 4–5 with 1 or 2 other dishes
300 g (11 oz) chicken breast
¾ teaspoon salt
1 egg white
450 g (1 lb) asparagus
6 tablespoons vegetable oil
3 slices root ginger, shredded
15 g (½ oz) butter
1 tablespoon light soy sauce
1 tablespoon oyster sauce
2 garlic cloves, peeled and crushed
2 tablespoons chicken stock
1 tablespoon white wine

Preparation time: 15 minutes
Cooking time: 11 minutes

This is a fresh-looking dish where the whiteness of the chicken contrasts well with the greenness of the asparagus.
1. Cut the chicken into triple matchstick-size slivers. Sprinkle with the salt, rubbing it in well, and brush all over with egg white. Trim off and discard 2.5 cm (1 inch) from the root end of the asparagus and cut each stem into two. Parboil for 5 minutes, then drain.
2. Heat the oil in a wok or frying pan, add the ginger and fry for 20 seconds. Add the chicken slivers. Turn them in the oil over a medium heat for 1½ minutes. Remove and drain.
3. Pour away half the excess oil in the pan. Add the butter and asparagus to the pan and turn a few times. Add the sauces, garlic, stock and wine. Stir-fry for 1½ minutes. Return the chicken slivers to the pan. Raise the heat to high and continue to stir-fry for 1½ minutes. Serve immediately.

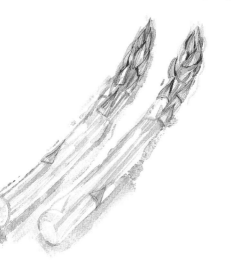

LEFT, Chinese roast chicken; RIGHT, Quick-fried slivers of chicken with asparagus

QUICK-FRIED DICED CHICKEN AND MUSHROOMS WITH CHICKEN LIVER AND CUCUMBER

SERVES 4–5 with 1 or 2 other dishes
250 g (9 oz) chicken breast
175 g (6 oz) chicken liver
2 teaspoons salt
1 egg white
5 tablespoons vegetable oil
175 g (6 oz) firm button mushrooms
15 g (½ oz) butter
1 tablespoon yellow bean sauce
2 garlic cloves, peeled and crushed
1½ teaspoons sugar
1 tablespoon chicken stock
1 tablespoon dark soy sauce
½ medium cucumber
1 tablespoon dry sherry

Preparation time: 15 minutes
Cooking time: 7–8 minutes

Here is a typically Chinese exercise in the orchestration of food textures. The cubes of chicken meat, liver, mushrooms and diced cucumber are cooked together over a high heat to produce a dish of considerable texture and flavour.

1. Cut the chicken breast and liver into 1 cm (½ inch) cubes. Rub with salt and brush all over with egg white.

2. Heat 4 tablespoons of the oil in a wok or frying pan. When hot, add the chicken and liver cubes. Stir-fry over a medium heat for 1½ minutes. Remove and set aside.

3. Cut the mushrooms into 1 cm (½ inch) cubes. Add the remaining oil to the wok or frying pan. When hot, add the mushrooms and stir-fry over a medium heat for 1 minute, then push them to one side of the pan. Add the butter to the other side and when melted, add the yellow bean sauce, garlic, sugar, stock and soy sauce and stir to make a creamy sauce.

4. Raise the heat to high. Return the chicken and liver cubes into the bubbling sauce and mix until evenly coated. Finally, cut the cucumber into 1 cm (½ inch) cubes and add to the pan. Stir-fry with the other ingredients for a few seconds, then sprinkle the sherry over and serve.

CUCUMBER
Cultivated for thousands of years, cucumber is a member of the squash family which is thought to have originated in India. Its cool, refreshing quality and its crispness make it a popular ingredient in Oriental cooking. It is also easy to cook, lending itself to fast cooking in a wok. It is, of course, excellent served raw, both as an ingredient in dishes and as a garnish. Pickled cucumber is a favourite Oriental pickle.

CRISPY SPICED CHICKEN DRUMSTICKS

SERVES 4–5 with 1 or 2 other dishes
8 chicken drumsticks
1 teaspoon salt
¾ teaspoon freshly ground black pepper
1 tablespoon yellow bean sauce
2 tablespoons light soy sauce
1 tablespoon hoisin sauce
1 tablespoon chilli sauce
2 tablespoons dry sherry
1 tablespoon sugar
3 slices root ginger, shredded
3 garlic cloves, peeled and crushed
3 spring onions, chopped
vegetable oil for deep-frying
sprigs fresh coriander, to garnish

Preparation time: 10 minutes, plus marinating
Cooking time: about 50 minutes

This dish makes a useful starter for a main meal and can also be used as a canapé or finger-food for a cocktail party.
1. Rub the drumsticks with the salt and pepper. Place them in a heat-proof basin. Mix the sauces with the sherry and sugar and pour over the drumsticks. Finally, sprinkle and rub them with the ginger, garlic and spring onion. Leave to marinate for a couple of hours.
2. Place the basin with the drumsticks in a steamer or a large saucepan with boiling water to come halfway up the sides of the basin. Steam for 10 minutes. Cover the top of the basin with a piece of kitchen foil and steam for a further 30 minutes.
3. Allow to cool slightly, then place the drumsticks in a wire basket and lower them into the hot oil to deep-fry for 7–8 minutes or until the outside is crispy.
4. Serve garnished with fresh coriander as a starter or as finger food.

CRISPY SKIN PEPPERED CHICKEN

SERVES 4–5 with 1 or 2 other dishes
1 × 1.5 kg (3½ lb) roasting chicken
1 tablespoon salt
¾ teaspoon freshly ground black pepper
3 slices root ginger, finely chopped
1 tablespoon light soy sauce
celery leaves, to garnish

Preparation time: 20 minutes, plus marinating overnight
Cooking time: 1½ hours
Oven: 200°C, 400°F, Gas Mark 6; then, 180°C, 350°F, Gas Mark 4

This dish is spicy, crispy in texture, yet light in colour. It is a good one to serve at a meal where the other dishes are stir- or soft-fried and given a darker colour by the use of soy sauce.
1. Wash and dry the chicken thoroughly inside and out. Mix the salt and pepper in a small, very dry saucepan. Turn and stir them over a low heat for 1½–2 minutes or until the mixture gives off a distinct peppery aroma. Remove from the heat and allow to cool, then rub the bird all over with the mixture. Reserve the excess.
2. Leave the chicken to marinate for a couple of hours.
3. Mix the ginger with the soy sauce until well blended, then rub all over the chicken. Leave the chicken to marinate in the refrigerator overnight

4. Rub the chicken all over once more with the remaining salt and pepper mixture. Leave to stand for a further 2–3 hours.
5. Place the chicken on a rack in a roasting pan and cook in a preheated, moderately hot oven for 30 minutes. Reduce the heat to moderate and roast for a further hour. Serve garnished with celery leaves.

LEFT, Crispy spiced chicken drumsticks; RIGHT, Crispy skin peppered chicken

SOY-BRAISED CHICKEN

4 tablespoons vegetable oil

3 tablespoons sugar

150 ml (5 fl oz) dark soy sauce

1.5 litres (2½ pints) water

1 large knob galangal, about 100 g (4 oz), bruised

1 large onion, peeled and sliced

1 tablespoon salt

3 stalks spring onions

1 chicken, about 1 kg (2 lb)

1 tablespoon cornflour

sliced cucumber or pineapple rings, to garnish

Preparation time: 15 minutes plus cooling

Cooking time: 1 hour 15 minutes

This hails from the south Chinese province of Guangdung from where most of the emigrés to South-East Asia came. Like many other rustic dishes, it first made its appearance as an itinerant hawker item. In time, the migrant Chinese, having got used to exotic spices, decided the humble dish was not good enough without some enhancement. This is the delicious result.

1. Heat the oil in a wok and add the sugar. Caramelize over a moderate heat till the mixture is tawny brown, then add the soy sauce and water.

2. Bring the mixture to the boil and add the galangal, onion, salt and spring onions. When the sauce boils again, add the chicken. Cover and cook for 35 minutes.

3. Switch off the heat and allow to cool completely, letting the chicken continue to cook in the residual heat.

4. When the dish is completely cold, lift the chicken out and drain. Return the sauce in the wok to the stove and bring back to the boil and reduce over a high heat for 30 minutes.

5. Add the cornflour, dissolved in a little water, to the sauce and cook till thick. Remove all solid matter with a slotted spoon and keep the sauce hot.

6. Cut the chicken into serving pieces the following way, using a Chinese cleaver or heavy knife: cut the chicken into half lengthwise. Slice around each leg and remove the largest bone. Chop through the cartilage into bite-sized pieces. Remove as much of the breast bone as you can and cut the breast meat into bite-sized pieces.

7. Reassemble the chicken pieces, skin side up, on a serving plate and garnish with sliced cucumber or pineapple rings. Serve the sauce separately. Bottled chilli sauce or mustard make good additional dips for the soy-braised chicken, which is meant to be served at room temperature with its own hot sauce.

CHICKEN CURRY

1 chicken, about 1.5 kg (3 lb)

6 tablespoons vegetable oil

½ onion, peeled and ground

2 tablespoons ginger, ground

2 tablespoons curry powder

350 ml (12 fl oz) coconut milk

200 ml (7 fl oz) water

2 large potatoes, peeled and quartered

1 tablespoon light soy sauce

½ teaspoon sugar

1 tablespoon lemon juice

chopped red chilli, to garnish

Preparation time: 20 minutes

Cooking time: 50 minutes

Curry in South-East Asia is not a single item for the word simply means 'spice blend' and there must be thousands of different curries between Bali and Bangkok. They can be as different from one another as chalk from cheese. Basically Indian, curry takes on many forms depending on where in South-East Asia it further evolved. The Thais like it brimming with fire, Indonesians perfume theirs with fresh herbs and Singaporeans put potatoes in theirs. Yes, the British had a hand in this one too.

1. Cut the chicken into 8 joints.

2. Heat the oil in a frying pan or wok and fry the onion and ginger till light brown. Add the curry powder, moistened with a little of the coconut milk, and fry over a low heat for 6 minutes. Transfer to a deep pot.

3. Add the rest of the coconut milk and the water and bring to the boil. Add the chicken and cook for 10 minutes, uncovered.

4. Now add the potatoes to the pot, then the soy sauce, sugar and lemon juice and cook for a further 25 minutes. Serve on a warmed plate, garnished with chopped red chillis. Boiled rice or bread can be served with this dish.

LEFT, Soy-braised chicken; RIGHT, Chicken curry

STEAMED OR DOUBLE-BOILED CHICKEN WITH CHINESE CABBAGE

SERVES 4–6 with 1 or 2 other dishes
1 × 1.5 kg (3½ lb) chicken
2 teaspoons salt
6–8 medium mushrooms
750 g (1½ lb) Chinese cabbage
5 slices root ginger
2 chicken stock cubes

Preparation time: 10 minutes
Cooking time: 2 hours 15 minutes

This is a big main-course dish, which is meant to be eaten with quantities of rice. A good dish for large families.

1. Parboil the chicken in boiling water with the salt for 5–6 minutes, skimming off any scum, then drain to remove any impurities. Soak the mushrooms in boiling water, then drain and remove the stems. Cut the cabbage into 5 cm (2 inch) thick slices.

2. Place the whole chicken on top of the mushrooms and ginger in a large, deep, heatproof bowl. Pour in just enough water to cover. Cover the top of the bowl tightly with a piece of kitchen foil. Place the bowl in a very large saucepan containing about 5 cm (2 inches) of water, which should not come more than halfway up the sides of the bowl. Bring to the boil, then simmer for 1 hour.

3. Lift out the chicken and place the sliced cabbage in the bottom of the bowl. Sprinkle the cabbage with the crumbled stock cubes, then place the chicken on top of the cabbage. Cover the bowl again tightly with foil. Return to the boil and simmer gently for another hour.

TROPICAL SWEET AND SOUR CHICKEN

225 g (8 oz) chicken breast
1 egg, lightly beaten
3 tablespoons cornflour
400 ml (14 fl oz) oil for deep-frying
6 garlic cloves, peeled and sliced
½ onion, peeled and sliced
10 pineapple cubes
2 red chillies, sliced
1 tomato, quartered

For the sauce:
1 tablespoon malt vinegar
1 tablespoon sugar
2 tablespoons tomato sauce
½ teaspoon salt
4 tablespoons pineapple juice
100 ml (3½ fl oz) water

Preparation time: 15 minutes
Cooking time: 15 minutes

Sweet and sour meat and poultry dishes in the tropics tend to be fiery with liberal doses of chilli. Appetites are sluggish in humid climates so chillies are needed to whip them up. Since we don't have this problem, reduce or leave out the chilli altogether, if you prefer.

1. Cut the chicken into bite-sized cubes and coat with the beaten egg. Toss the pieces lightly in the cornflower.

2. Heat the oil to 180°C/350°F in a wok or frying pan and deep-fry the chicken till golden brown, about 4 minutes. Remove the chicken and all but 3 tablespoons of oil from the pan, reheat and fry the garlic and onion till light brown. Add the pineapple, chillies and tomato and stir-fry for a minute.

3. Combine all the sauce ingredients and add to the pan, together with the chicken. Cook for 1 or 2 minutes till the sauce is thick and has a nice glaze.

LEFT, Steamed or double-boiled chicken with Chinese cabbage; RIGHT, Tropical sweet and sour chicken

COLONIAL CHICKEN STEW

8 chicken drumsticks
2 tablespoons dark soy sauce
4 tablespoons vegetable oil
1 large onion, peeled and quartered
450 g (1 lb) potatoes, peeled and quartered
225 g (8 oz) carrots, diced
900 ml (1½ pints) water
5 cm (2 inch) piece cinnamon
5 cloves
10 peppercorns
2 teaspoons salt
2 teaspoons cornflour

Preparation time: 10 minutes
Cooking time: 35 minutes

This dish's name, and the potatoes in it, indicate that it is a typical cross-breed of the East and British colonial taste. Easy to prepare, it has a flavour that speaks of tiffin under waving palms on a white sandy beach with gin sling to wash it down.

1. Rub the chicken well on all sides with the soy sauce.
2. Heat the oil in a wok or frying pan and fry the onion for 2 minutes over a high heat.

3. Add the potatoes, carrots and chicken and stir well for 2 minutes. Add water, cinnamon, cloves, peppercorns, salt and cornflour and give them a good stir. Simmer for 30 minutes over a moderate heat.
4. Turn the stew into a warmed serving dish and serve it at once, perhaps with bread and butter.

Variation: Leave potatoes out of the stew but serve the dish with lots of separately cooked mashed potatoes to soak up the stew's plentiful sauce.

COCONUT-GRILLED CHICKEN

300 ml (½ pint) coconut milk
2 teaspoons turmeric powder
1 teaspoon chilli powder
2 tablespoons ground onions
1 tablespoon ground ginger
4 lime leaves
2 teaspoons salt
1 teaspoon sugar
1 chicken, about 1.5 kg (3 lb)

Preparation time: 10 minutes
Cooking time: 1 hour 25 minutes
Oven: 220°C, 425°F, Gas Mark 7; then, 180°C, 350°F, Gas Mark 4

LEFT, Colonial chicken stew; RIGHT, Coconut-grilled chicken

A delicious way to prepare chicken, especially when entertaining, this also looks attractive with its golden yellow colour. Lime leaves have a heady perfume and combine well with ginger and chilli.

1. Combine the coconut milk and all other ingredients except the chicken in a large pan and bring to the boil. Add the chicken and simmer over a moderate heat for 10 minutes until well coated and partially cooked. Turn it once or twice.
2. Remove the chicken from the pan and drain. Transfer it to a preheated hot oven for 30 minutes. When the skin begins to char a little, reduce the oven temperature to moderate and roast for another 45 minutes. If the wing and leg tips char too much, wrap them in silver foil. Baste the chicken liberally with coconut sauce several times while roasting.
3. Remove the chicken from the oven and allow to rest for a few minutes before either serving it whole to be carved at the table, or cut up into large joints and served on a large plate. The sauce should be reheated and served separately.

BRAISED QUAIL IN GINGER WINE

3 tablespoons lard
8 quail, dressed
1 tablespoon chopped ginger
2 stalks spring onions
4 tablespoons ginger wine
2 tablespoons sesame oil
1 teaspoon salt
1 teaspoon pepper
1 teaspoon sugar
1 tablespoon dark soy sauce
900 ml (1½ pints) water
spring onion tassles, to garnish

Preparation time: 10 minutes
Cooking time: 55 minutes

These little game birds have always been symbolic of plenty, at least where their eggs are concerned as the Chinese consume vast numbers of them, pickled, salted or simply boiled. Inexpensive, a pair of quail when braised make a substantial and delicious main course for one. As the meat is on the dry side, this recipe is a good way of cooking them.

1. Heat the lard in a large frying pan or wok over a moderate heat and brown the quail all over. Remove and set aside.
2. Put the ginger and whole spring onions into the pan and fry for 2 minutes. Add the ginger wine, sesame oil, salt, pepper, sugar and soy sauce and transfer to a large enough pot to contain all eight quail.
3. Add the water and bring to the boil. Add the quail, cover the pan tightly and braise for 35 minutes over a moderate heat. When done, remove the quail and set aside until ready to serve, allowing two quail per person, and garnishing each serving with a spring onion tassle.
4. Reduce the gravy by boiling it down for 15 minutes. Pour about 3 tablespoons of gravy on each serving, putting any left over in a jug for serving separately.

STIR-FRIED CHICKEN WITH WALNUTS

150 ml (5 fl oz) water
225 g (8 oz) chicken breast meat
3 tablespoons vegetable oil
2 garlic cloves, peeled and crushed
1 tablespoon yellow bean sauce
½ tablespoon pepper
100 g (4 oz) shelled, skinned walnuts
1 stalk spring onion, chopped

Preparation time: 10 minutes, plus cooling
Cooking time: 10 minutes

Chicken breast meat has a great compatibility with members of the nut family. A great standby, this tasty dish takes but a few minutes to toss together if you have a store cupboard of ingredients to hand.

The trick is to poach the chicken in just a little water and use up the stock during the stir-fry for a more flavoursome dish.

1. Bring the water to the boil in a saucepan and poach the chicken for 5 minutes. Remove the chicken from the pan, reserving the stock. Cool and cut into cubes.
2. Heat the oil in a pan and fry the garlic till light brown. Add the bean sauce and pepper and stir for 30 seconds. Add the chicken and reserved stock and stir over a high heat for 2 minutes. Toss in the walnuts and give the pan a good stir to blend them with other ingredients.
3. Just before dishing up, toss in the chopped spring onions.

LEFT, Braised quail in ginger wine; RIGHT, Stir-fried chicken with walnuts

SHREDDED SPICED DUCK

1 duck, about 2 kg (4½ lb)
2 litres (3½ pints) water
5 candlenuts
½ large onion, peeled and chopped
10 peppercorns
4 garlic cloves, peeled
1 thumb-sized piece galangal
2 slices ginger
1 teaspoon shrimp paste
1 teaspoon salt
2 tablespoons lemon juice
200 ml (7 fl oz) coconut milk
1 teaspoon sugar
cucumber slices, to garnish

Preparation time: 15 minutes
Cooking time: 1½ hours

Free-range ducks in Southeast Asia are not known for their tender succulence. In Indonesia, especially, where buffalo, mutton and wild boar have to be tenderised in various ways, tough birds get the same bashing treatment. What results is a pâté-like consistency, whatever meat is cooked, and something quite delicious.

1. Boil the duck in the water, in a covered saucepan for 45 minutes over a moderate heat. Remove the duck, cool and bone it completely. Reserve the duck stock.
2. With a mallet, or the blunt edge of a cleaver, gently pound the duck meat until it is well shredded.
3. Grind together in a mortar or blender the candlenuts, onion, peppercorns, garlic, galangal, ginger and shrimp paste.

4. Combine the salt, lemon juice, coconut milk, duck stock (about 200ml/7 fl oz) and sugar in a wok or frying pan and bring to the boil. Add the ground spices and duck meat and cook, stirring all the time, till almost dry. Adjust the seasoning if necessary. Turn on to a warmed platter and garnish with sliced cucumber, the traditional accompaniment for this dish. Serve with plain boiled rice.

CORIANDER DUCK

1 oven-ready duck
3 tablespoons coriander powder
3 tablespoons dark soy sauce
2 tablespoons sugar
1 tablespoon salt
1 teaspoon black pepper
5 tablespoons vegetable oil
3 garlic cloves, chopped
1 stalk fresh coriander, chopped
2 litres (3½ pints) water
sprigs fresh coriander, to garnish

Preparation time: 15 minutes plus cooling
Cooking time: 2 hours 15 minutes

This is an excellent way to cook duck, with its fat being tempered with spices. It's a tropical variation of Cantonese soy-braised duck with a generous infusion of both powdered and fresh chopped coriander.

1. Rub the duck all over with the coriander powder, dark soy sauce, sugar, salt and pepper and leave in a deep bowl.
2. Heat the oil in a flame proof casserole or wok and fry the garlic till brown. Add the chopped coriander and fry for 1 minute. Put the duck in the pan and brown all over.
3. Scrape the marinade from the bowl and add it to the water. Pour this mixture over the duck and braise, covered, over a moderate heat for 1¾ hours, checking every half an hour or so and topping up with more water, if necessary. (The rate of evaporation depends on the utensil you use; a wok, with its curved shape, is ideal for cradling the duck. Your lid should be tight fitting.)

4. When cooked, the gravy should be thick with an attractive glaze. Remove the duck to cool and reduce the gravy over high heat for 15 minutes, adjusting the seasoning, if necessary. Set the gravy aside to cool, then skim off the fat. Reheat and transfer to a gravy boat, chop up the duck and serve on a warmed platter, garnished with coriander sprigs, with the gravy served separately.

LEFT, Shredded spiced duck; RIGHT, Coriander duck

AROMATIC CRISPY DUCK

SERVES 5–6 with 1 or 2 other dishes
1 × 2 kg (4½ lb) duck
2 teaspoons salt
⅓ teaspoon freshly ground black pepper
⅓ teaspoon Chinese 'five-spice powder' (optional)
4 slices root ginger
4 spring onions
2 tablespoons dark soy sauce
1 tablespoon clear honey
1 tablespoon vinegar
1 tablespoon hoisin sauce
vegetable oil for deep-frying

For the sauce:
2 tablespoons vegetable oil
6 tablespoons yellow bean sauce
3 tablespoons sugar
1 tablespoon sesame oil

Preparation time: 25 minutes, plus marinating overnight and cooling
Cooking time: 1 hour 30 minutes

This excellent party dish can be prepared the day before it is wanted and only needs to be deep-fried for 8–10 minutes just before serving.
1. Clean the duck thoroughly and rub it inside and out with salt, pepper, and five-spice powder, if used. Wrap the duck in foil and leave to marinate overnight in the refrigerator.
2. Shred the ginger, and cut the spring onions into 4 cm (1½ inch) lengths. Stuff half the ginger and spring onion into the cavity of the duck and place the other half on top of the bird.
3. Put the duck, still wrapped in foil, into a heatproof dish or bowl, place into a steamer and steam vigorously for 1¼ hours. Remove the duck from the steamer, allow it to cool and unwrap the foil. Combine the soy sauce, honey, vinegar, and hoisin sauce and use to brush the duck all over. Leave the duck to stand for 1 or 2 hours in an airy place, to allow it to dry.

4. Heat the oil in a deep-fryer to 180°–190°C/350°–375°F, or until a cube of bread browns in 30 seconds. Place the duck in a wire basket and lower it into the hot oil to deep-fry for 9–10 minutes over moderate heat.
5. For the sauce; heat the oil in a small saucepan. Add the yellow bean sauce and stir over a low heat for 1½ minutes. Add the sugar and stir for 1½ minutes. Add the sesame oil and continue to stir for 1 further minute. Allow the sauce to stand and cool.
6. Serve the duck cut up into bite-sized pieces, with lettuce leaves for wrapping the meat in together with some shredded cucumber and spring onion. Brush the duck liberally with the sauce before wrapping in the leaves.

SZECHUAN QUICK-FRIED RIBBON OF DUCK IN HOT BLACK BEAN SAUCE

250 g (9 oz) roast duck meat
5 slices root ginger
100 g (4 oz) young leeks, trimmed
1 red sweet pepper
2 red chilli peppers
1 dried green chilli pepper
1 tablespoon salted black beans
2 garlic cloves, peeled and crushed
4 tablespoons vegetable oil
1½ tablespoons sugar
1 tablespoon vinegar
2 tablespoons dry sherry
2 tablespoons butter

Preparation time: 20 minutes
Cooking time: 7 minutes

An effective and quickly cooked way of dealing with duck, this recipe comes from China's Szechuan province.
1. Cut the duck along the grain of the meat into double matchstick strips. Cut the ginger and leeks into similar-sized strips. Seed and chop the sweet and chilli peppers. Soak the beans in water for 5 minutes, then drain and mash with the garlic.
2. Heat the oil in a wok or frying pan. When hot, add the ginger, leeks, and sweet and chilli peppers and stir-fry over medium heat for 2 minutes. Add the duck strips, sprinkle with salt, and stir-fry all the ingredients in the pan for 1–2 minutes. Remove from the pan and set aside.

3. Add the butter to the pan. When it has melted add the black beans mashed with the garlic. Stir-fry for 15 seconds. Add the sugar, and pour in the soy sauce, vinegar and dry sherry. Stir well to mix.
4. Return the duck meat, leeks and peppers to the pan, and mix quickly with the bubbling sauce. Stir-fry over a high heat for 1 minute.

FROM THE TOP, Aromatic crispy duck; Szechuan quick-fried ribbons of duck in hot black bean sauce

PEKING DUCK

SERVES 4–6 with 1 or 2 other dishes
1 × 2 kg (4½ lb) duck
6 spring onions
1 medium cucumber

For the sauce:
4 tablespoons vegetable oil
8 tablespoons yellow bean sauce
4 tablespoons sugar
1 teaspoon sesame oil

For the pancakes:
450 g (1 lb) plain flour
½ teaspoon sugar
1 teaspoon vegetable oil
300 ml (½ pint) water
a little sesame oil

Preparation time: about 50 minutes, plus drying overnight and cooling
Cooking time: 2 hours
Oven: 200°C, 400°F, Gas Mark 6

The restaurant where Peking Duck was first commercially produced in 1864 was called Chuan Chu Te (Congregation of All Virtues). It is now more than 10 times its original size and simply called the Peking Duck Restaurant. Kenneth Lo spent more than an hour in their kitchen filming their cooking during one of his gastronomic tours of China and was surprised to find that they roasted the bird for only 35 minutes at the very high temperature of 250°C, 485°F, Gas Mark 9. In his experience the roasting time seems much too short to produce the crispiest duck skin. At Kenneth Lo's own restaurant duck is roasted at 200°C, 400°F, Gas Mark 6 for precisely twice as long – 70–80 minutes depending on size – which seems to produce better results.

1. Clean and dry the duck thoroughly. Hang it up in a dry airy place for 5 hours or overnight to dry out the skin. Cut the spring onions into 7.5 cm (3 inch) lengths, splitting the thicker lengths in two. Cut the cucumber into similar-sized strips.
2. Place the duck on a rack in a roasting pan and roast in a preheated oven for 1¼ hours or until the duck is cooked through and crisp. Do not open the oven door during cooking.
3. To make the sauce, heat the oil in a small saucepan, add the yellow bean sauce and stir over a low heat for 2 minutes. Add the sugar and sesame oil and stir for a further 1½ minutes. Leave to cool for 20–30 minutes.
4. To make the pancakes, sift the flour into a mixing bowl. Stir in the sugar, vegetable oil and the warm water. Stir and mix with a pair of chopsticks or wooden spoon until thoroughly combined. Knead the mixture to a firm dough and form into two large sausage-shaped strips. Cut each strip into 12 slices and form each piece into a small ball. Flatten each ball with the palm of the

hand into a round flat disc on a board or work surface.
5. Brush the top surface of one of the discs with sesame oil and place a second disc flat on top of it to form a sandwich. Using a small rolling pin, roll the sandwich into a pancake of about 10–13 cm (4–5 inch) diameter. Repeat until all the dough has been used.
6. Heat a dry frying pan over a low to medium heat. When hot, place a double-pancake sandwich flat on the pan and shake so that the pancake slides over the surface. After 1½ minutes turn the pancake over with a fish slice to cook on the opposite side. After just over 1 minute, the pancake will begin to puff and bubble slightly. It is ready when brown spots begin to appear on the underside.
7. Remove from the pan and gently peel the sandwich apart into two pancakes. Fold each pancake in half, with the soft side on the inside, and stack them up. If they are not to be used immediately, cover them with a damp cloth (they can be reheated when required in a steamer in a couple of minutes). For people who do not wish to go to the trouble of making them, pancakes are often available in packs of 10 or 12 from Chinese food stores or supermarkets.
8. Cut the duck skin and meat off the carcase in thin slices about the size of a 10p piece and serve separately. Eat the duck wrapped in a pancake, which is first of all brushed with 'duck sauce' and liberally sprinkled with spring onions and shredded cucumber. What is particularly appealing about eating roast duck in this manner is that for every bite and mouthful you will enjoy the aromatic texture of the crackling duck skin, the savoury tenderness of the duck meat, the plummy piquancy of the sauce and the fresh crunchiness of the vegetables.

EIGHT-TREASURE ROAST GOOSE

SERVES 6–8 with 1 or 2 other dishes
1 oven-ready goose, about 3–4 kg (7–9 lb)

The Eight Treasures:
8 chestnuts
8 medium Chinese dried mushrooms
175 g (6 oz) glutinous rice
2 Chinese wind-dried sausages, cut into 1 cm
    (½ inch) pieces
4 tablespoons lotus nuts
6 tablespoons chopped bamboo shoots
    (chopped to pea-size)
7 tablespoons Chinese roast pork, chopped
    into 2 cm (¾ inch) cubes
5 tablespoons cubed ham, cut into same sized
    pieces as the pork

Additional ingredients:
4 tablespoons vegetable oil
4 slices root ginger, roughly chopped
2 spring onions, roughly chopped
2 tablespoons light soy sauce
2 teaspoons sugar
3 tablespoons dry sherry

Preparation time: about 50 minutes, plus drying, cooling and soaking
Cooking time: 2 hours 35 minutes
Oven: 200°C, 400°F, Gas Mark 6; then, 180°C, 350°F, Gas Mark 4

As in England, goose is a traditional bird in China which appears on the dinner table only on special occasions. Now that Peking Duck has become such an established dish for banquets and party meals, roast goose is increasing in popularity as an alternative. As goose is a larger bird than duck it often appears on the table on bigger occasions. Roast goose can be prepared and cooked in precisely the same manner as Peking Duck, but it is more often boned and stuffed with eight ingredients known as the 'Eight Treasures'. In China, eight is considered an auspicious number for its well-balanced completeness. Hence the Eight Fairies who crossed the sea; the Eight Famous Horses of Emperor Tai-Chung of Tang Dynasty.

1. Bone the goose (see page 137) and leave to stand in an airy place to dry for 4–5 hours.
2. To make the Eight Treasure stuffing, slash the chestnuts and boil them for 30 minutes. Allow them to cool, then remove the skins. Boil the chestnut meats for a further 20 minutes in fresh water. Meanwhile, soak the dried mushrooms in boiling water for 30 minutes. Drain, remove the stems, and cut the caps into quarters.
3. Boil the rice for 8 minutes, then drain.
4. Heat the oil in a wok or large frying pan. When hot, add the ginger, mushrooms, spring onions and Chinese sausage. Stir-fry over a medium heat for 1½ minutes. Add the chestnuts, lotus nuts and bamboo shoots. Stir-fry for 2 minutes.
6. Add the glutinous rice. Turn and mix the rice with all the other ingredients, allowing time for the rice to heat through completely. Add the soy sauce and sugar and sprinkle with sherry. Stir-fry until all the ingredients are evenly mixed. Remove from the heat and allow to cool slightly, then use to stuff the cavity of the goose. Sew up the cavity securely.
7. Place the stuffed goose on a rack set in a roasting pan. Roast in a preheated hot oven for 1 hour. Reduce the heat to moderate and continue to roast for 30 minutes, until the goose and stuffing are cooked through. Because of the expansion of the stuffings inside the cavity, the goose should appear quite round and puffed up and the skin should be quite brown and crispy. Cut into even slices with a sharp knife and reassemble, if possible, into its original shape. Serve in the centre of the table for the diners to help themselves.

FISH

The emphasis here is very much on fresh sea fish and shellfish, in a tantalising array of recipes culled from the best of Oriental fish cookery. There is Szechuan crispy whole fish from China, Prawn satay from Singapore and Fish bergadel as a reminder of European influences on Far Eastern cookery.

Prawn satay (see page 92)

SZECHUAN CRISPY WHOLE FISH IN HOT 'TOU PAN' SAUCE

SERVES 4–5 with 1 or 2 other dishes
3 slices root ginger, shredded and chopped
1 teaspoon salt
vegetable oil for deep-frying
1 kg (2¼ lb) fish (carp, perch or pike)
3 tablespoons plain flour
3 spring onions, trimmed
4 tablespoons lard
2 rashers bacon, rinded and chopped
25 g (1 oz) Szechuan Ja-Chai pickle, chopped
25 g (1 oz) Chinese Snow Pickle, chopped
   (optional)
1 small green pepper, seeded and cut into
   strips
1 small red pepper, seeded and cut into
   strips
2 chilli peppers, seeded and shredded
1 tablespoon sugar
1 tablespoon yellow bean sauce
2 tablespoons dark soy sauce
2 tablespoons chicken stock
2 tablespoons dry sherry
1 tablespoon cornflour mixed with 4
   tablespoons water

Preparation time: 20 minutes
Cooking time: 13–14 minutes

The attraction of this dish lies in the contrast of flavour between the rich spiciness of this well-known Szechuan sauce and the chunky meatiness of the fish.

1. Mix the ginger with the salt and 1 tablespoon of the oil. Rub the fish inside and out with this mixture, then dust with 2 tablespoons of the flour.

2. Heat the oil to 180°C/350°F, or until a cube of bread browns in 30 seconds, in a deep-sided frying-pan. When hot, lower in the fish and deep-fry for 6–7 minutes. Remove and drain.

3. Cut the spring onions into 2.5 cm (1 inch) lengths.

4. Heat the lard in a wok or a frying pan. When hot add the spring onions, bacon, pickles and sweet and chilli peppers. Stir-fry over a high heat for 2 minutes. Add the sugar, sauces, stock and sherry and stir-fry

for a further 1½ minutes. Slowly pour in the blended cornflour, to thicken the sauce. Lower the fish into the sauce to cook for 2 minutes on either side, basting as you cook. Reduce the heat to low and cook for 1 further minute.

5. Transfer the whole fish to a heated serving dish. Pour the sauce and vegetables over it and serve immediately.

CHILLIES IN ORIENTAL COOKERY
Chilli peppers are used extensively in Szechuan cooking. Red chilli peppers tend to be milder than green (less ripe) ones, since they become milder in flavour as they ripen. Both colours are, however, still hot and spicy and fresh ones should be handled with care, since they can sting the skin. Never rub your eyes or touch your face if you have been handling them and wash your hands once you have finished with them.

Dried red chillies are often used to season the oil for stir-frying: remove the seeds once the oil is heated if a less hot and spicy dish is required.

Chilli paste, made from chillies, soya beans, salt, flour and sugar, is also used as a flavouring; red chilli powder is an acceptable substitute.

STEAMED SEA BASS

1 kg (2 lb) sea bass
1½ teaspoons salt
5 slices root ginger
6 tablespoons vegetable oil
4 spring onions, trimmed
2 tablespoons light soy sauce
¼ tablespoon freshly ground black pepper
2 tablespoons dry sherry
lime slices, to garnish

Preparation time: 20 minutes
Cooking time: 10 minutes

The 'searing' of fish in this recipe, by pouring a stream of sizzling hot oil over it after it has been steamed, but just before serving, is not unlike the French method of flambéeing food.

1. Clean the fish inside and out, and rub with a mixture of the salt, ginger and 1 tablespoon of the oil. Cut the spring onions into 2.5 cm (1 inch) lengths. Place the fish on a heatproof dish and pile half the ginger and spring onion down the length of the fish.

2. Place the dish in a steamer and steam vigorously for 20 minutes. Discard the ginger and spring onion and drain off any excess water which may have accumulated in the dish. Pour the soy sauce, pepper and sherry down the length of the fish and lay the remaining spring onion and ginger over it.

3. Bring the fish to the table partly covered in spring onion and shredded ginger and garnished with slices of lime. Heat the remaining oil in a small saucepan or frying pan until smoking. Pour the hot oil slowly through the layer of ginger and spring onion over the length of the fish: this helps to seal in the fresh flavour of the ginger and onion.

TROPICAL SWEET & SOUR COD

450 g (1 lb) cod fillets
4 tablespoons cornflour
2 teaspoons salt
400 ml (14 fl oz) plus 3 tablespoons vegetable oil
½ onion, peeled and diced
2 garlic cloves, peeled and sliced
2 red chillies, sliced
1 tomato, quartered
10 pineapple chunks

For the sauce:
1 tablespoon malt vinegar
2 tablespoons tomato sauce
1 tablespoon sugar
200 ml (7 fl oz) pineapple juice
1 teaspoon salt

Preparation time: 20 minutes
Cooking time: 15 minutes

Transplanted by Chinese emigrants from China to the tropics, this dish has undergone a tangy transformation but still reflects the universal Yin Yang harmony with a fiery infusion of chillies and the tang of pineapples.

1. Cut the cod fillets into 2.5 cm (1 inch) square pieces, 1 cm (½ inch) thick. Place in a plastic bag together with the cornflour and salt. Give the bag a good shake till the fish is well coated.

2. Heat the 400 ml (14 fl oz) of oil in a wok or frying pan to 180°C/350°F, or until a cube of bread browns in 30 seconds. Fry the fish, a few pieces at a time, till golden brown. Drain on absorbent kitchen paper and keep warm.

3. In a clean pan, heat the 3 tablespoons of oil and fry the onion, garlic and chillies for 1 minute over a high heat. Add the tomato and pineapple and cook, stirring for another minute.

4. Combine the sauce ingredients and add to the pan. Bring to the boil and add the fish. Give the pan a good stir for 1 minute then transfer the food to a warmed plate and serve hot.

FROM THE TOP, Steamed sea bass; Tropical sweet and sour cod

NANYANG STEAMED FISH

1 sea bass, about 1 kg (2¼ lb)
2 teaspoons salt
3 tablespoons lard
5 shallots, peeled and sliced
½ teaspoon black pepper
2 tablespoons light soy sauce
1 tablespoon sesame oil

To garnish:
1 small bunch fresh coriander leaves
lemon twists

Preparation time: 20 minutes
Cooking time: 25 minutes

This is one of the few dishes the migrant Chinese brought with them to their new home of 'Nanyang' – 'South Seas' in the Chinese argot – that escaped a spicy make-over, though not entirely, since fried shallots and fresh coriander leaves were added. There was an inherent snobbery among the migrant Chinese, who referred to their 'sin-keh' (newly-arrived) relatives as 'bumkins', alluding to their own sophis-tication in speaking English; hence, the spicing-up of a traditional dish just to make a point of their 'elevated' status!

1. Gut and scale the sea bass, washing the stomach and gill cavity to remove all traces of blood.

2. Make two or three diagonal cuts along both sides of the fish almost to the bone. Rub all over with salt. Place in a deep dish in a steamer or in a saucepan with water to come half way up the sides of the dish and steam for 25 minutes.

3. While the fish is steaming, heat the lard in a wok or frying pan and fry the shallots till brown. Add the pepper, soy sauce and sesame oil and give it a good stir. Transfer to a small bowl and keep warm.

4. When the fish is done, transfer it to a warmed serving plate, pour the shallot mixture over and garnish with sprigs of coriander and lemon twists.

SPICY SESAME-BRAISED FISH

450 g (1 lb) catfish
1 teaspoon salt
6 tablespoons vegetable oil
3 garlic cloves, peeled and sliced
1 tablespoon ginger, chopped
1 teaspoon black peppercorns, crushed
2 tablespoons sesame oil
1 tablespoon dark soy sauce
1 teaspoon sugar
2 teaspoons cornflour
275 ml (9 fl oz) water
2 stalks spring onions, chopped

Preparation time: 20 minutes
Cooking time: 20 minutes

FROM THE TOP, Nanyang steamed fish; Spicy sesame-braised fish

When fat, slithery catfish entangle their lethal spines in a fishing net, they are swooped upon with cries of joy. Extremely tricky denizens of the deep to deal with, catfish have a delicious taste and texture quite unlike most other fish. If catfish is not available use similar fish like conger eel, monkfish or halibut in this dish: it's the sauce that counts.

1. If the fishmonger has not deboned the fish, cook it on the bone. Cut into 2.5 cm (1 inch) thick chunks. Rub with salt and set aside.

2. Heat the oil in a wok or frying pan till smoking and fry the fish, a few chunks at a time, till the outside is well-sealed and the fish is partly cooked.

3. Remove the fish from the pan with a slotted spoon and also drain off and discard half the oil. Fry the garlic and ginger till light brown in the remaining oil. Add the peppercorns, sesame oil, soy sauce, sugar and cornflour dissolved in the water.

4. Bring the contents of the pan to the boil, stirring as it thickens, and add the fried fish. Simmer for 5 minutes. Add the chopped spring onions in the last minute and give the pan a good stir.

5. Transfer the fish in its sauce to a warmed serving plate and serve it immediately.

FISH BERGEDEL

175 g (6 oz) cod
450 g (1 lb) mashed potatoes
4 tablespoons soft white breadcrumbs
1 tablespoon coriander powder
½ teaspoon pepper
2 teaspoons salt
1 tablespoon onion, peeled and chopped
1 egg, lightly beaten
400 ml (14 fl oz) vegetable oil

Preparation time: 20 minutes, plus cooling
Cooking time: 20 minutes

When the Dutch and Portuguese brought their potato-eating habit to South-East Asia, it rubbed off on the natives, bergedel being a mutant of the Dutch 'frikadeller' – potato and meat ball. Bergedel are often used as dumplings in spicy chicken soup. The glorious tradition of 'rijstaffel' or 'rice table' is also a Dutch-minted word, though most of the dishes are of Indian origin. These can number some three dozen curries, sambals, chutneys and side dishes eaten with rice.

1. Poach the cod in sufficient water to cover for 5 minutes. Drain, cool and flake well.
2. Mix with all the other ingredients except the oil in a large bowl and blend well. Using floured hands, shape the mixture into balls, each the size of a plum but slightly flattened.
3. Heat the oil in a deep pan to 180°C/350°F, or until a cube of bread browns in 30 seconds. Deep-fry three or four bergedel at a time till golden brown.
4. Drain on absorbent kitchen paper and serve hot or cold with sliced cucumber.

TAMARIND FISH CURRY

2 tablespoons tamarind paste
500 ml (18 fl oz) water
350 g (12 oz) halibut
1 stalk lemon grass, sliced from 5 cm (2 inch) of thick end
½ large onion, peeled and quartered
1 teaspoon turmeric powder
2 red chillies
1 teaspoon shrimp paste
4 tablespoons vegetable oil
1 tablespoon light soy sauce
1 teaspoon sugar
1 stalk lemon grass, bruised
1 tomato, quartered

Preparation time: 15 minutes, plus soaking
Cooking time: 12 minutes

The range of spicy seafood dishes in the spectrum of South-East Asian cooking is incredibly wide and tamarind is the liquid basis for most of them. (Coconut milk is another, but for mostly for meat and poultry dishes.) Though tamarind in paste form is relatively easy to obtain, lemon juice makes a tangy substitute, and will give a lighter sauce: use 1 tablespoon of concentrated juice for 1 tablespoon of tamarind paste and the same amount of water.

1. Dissolve the tamarind in the water and strain through a fine sieve. Discard the pith.
2. Cut the halibut into thick chunks and leave to soak in the tamarind liquid.
3. Grind together in a mortar or blender the lemon grass, onion, turmeric, chillies and shrimp paste.
4. Heat the oil in a wok or frying pan and fry the ground spices for 3 minutes over a moderate heat. Strain the tamarind liquid off the fish and add two-thirds of it to the pan, with the soy sauce, sugar, bruised lemon grass and tomato. Bring to the boil.
5. Add the fish and cook for 2 minutes. Check the seasoning and add the remaining tamarind liquid, if necessary.

LEFT, Fish bergedel; RIGHT, Tamarind fish curry

PRAWN SATAY WITH PEANUT SAUCE

24 large uncooked prawns, shelled
2 tablespoons coriander powder
1 tablespoon cumin powder
1 teaspoon turmeric powder
1 teaspoon chilli powder
½ onion, peeled and ground
1 tablespoon sugar
2 tablespoons salt
8 bamboo skewers

For the Peanut Sauce:
2 stalks lemon grass
½ large onion, peeled and sliced
1 teaspoon chilli powder
1 teaspoon shrimp paste
1 teaspoon salt
4 tablespoons vegetable oil
1 tablespoon sugar
1 tablespoon tamarind paste
250 ml (8 fl oz) water
175 g (6 oz) peanuts, ground

Preparation time: 35 minutes, plus marinating
Cooking time: 4 minutes per skewer, and 7 minutes for the sauce

Satay, also spelt 'saté', best reflects South-East Asian cooking. It certainly is the most ubiquitous, sold by itinerant hawkers on the beach in Bali and in supermarkets and restaurants from London to New York. Satay is basically spiced marinated meat or seafood on skewers, grilled and served with traditional peanut sauce. History has it that satay is called thus because the word in Chinese means 'three pieces', being the number of chunks on each skewer.

1. Slit each prawn down the back and remove the dark vein. Wash and dry.
2. Combine all the spice powders with the onion, sugar and salt and coat the prawns in the mixture. Set aside for 30 minutes for the prawns to absorb the flavours.
3. Meanwhile, make the peanut sauce. Slice the lemon grass, using only 5 cm (2 inch) of the thick bulb end. Place with all the other ingredients, except the oil, sugar, tamarind paste, water, and peanuts in a blender and grind till fine.
4. Heat the oil till it is smoking and fry the ground mixture over a medium heat for 3 minutes.

5. Dissolve the tamarind in water and strain. Add it to the pan with the salt, sugar and ground peanuts and cook for 4 minutes over a low heat, stirring constantly to prevent lumps. Adjust the seasoning, if necessary, and turn into a bowl.
6. Curl each prawn and place three on each skewer through the tail end and the thickest part. Press any left-over spice mixture on to the prawns and grill over a charcoal fire or under a preheated grill for 4 minutes, turning once.

PRAWN SAMBAL

300 g (11 oz) uncooked prawns
5 tablespoons vegetable oil
2 large onions, peeled and finely sliced
3 fresh red chillies
1 stalk lemon grass
2 garlic cloves, peeled
1 teaspoon shrimp paste
6 candlenuts
2 tomatoes, quartered
2 teaspoons salt   1 teaspoon sugar
1 tablespoon lemon juice
120 ml (4 fl oz) water

Preparation time: 20 minutes
Cooking time: 8 minutes

The word 'sambal' is of Indian origin and refers to any chilli-hot dish in a thick spice paste. It was daily fare for the Indian dockside workers in the newly founded British trading post of Singapore and for the trappers in Malayan rubber estates. Their Chinese co-workers must have found them tongue-searing at first but were soon cooking their own, less fiery, versions, with subtle hints of lemon.

1. Shell and clean the prawns and set aside until required.
2. Heat the oil in a wok or frying pan until smoking and fry one of the sliced onions till soft.

3. Grind together in a mortar or blender the red chillies, lemon grass, garlic, remaining onion, shrimp paste and candlenuts, and add to the pan.
4. Add the tomatoes and prawns and cook for another minute.
5. Add salt, sugar, lemon juice and water and cook for a further 2 minutes. Transfer to a warmed platter and serve with plain boiled rice.

FROM THE TOP, Prawn satay with peanut sauce; Prawn sambal

GINGER AND SPRING ONION CRAB

1 boiled crab, about 1.25 kg (2¾ lb), cleaned
    and chopped through the shell into large
    bite-sized pieces
3 tablespoons sherry
3 tablespoons soy sauce
2 tablespoons cornflour
4 tablespoons vegetable oil
4 slices root ginger, peeled and finely chopped
4 spring onions, finely chopped
1 teaspoon salt
2 teaspoons sugar

Preparation time: 20 minutes
Cooking time: about 5 minutes

1. Place the crab in pieces in a bowl, add 2 tablespoons sherry, 2 tablespoons soy sauce and the cornflour. Turn the pieces until well coated.
2. Heat the oil in a wok or frying pan until smoking, then add the crab and fry for about 1 minute. Add the ginger, spring onions, salt, sugar, remaining sherry and soy sauce. Stir-fry on a high heat for about 3 minutes, stirring all the time. Add a little water if the mixture becomes very dry.
3. Transfer the crab pieces to a warm serving dish and pour over the sauce.

STEAMED SCALLOPS IN BLACK BEAN SAUCE

12 scallops, on their shells
2 tablespoons vegetable oil
2 tablespoons salted black beans, soaked,
    drained and crushed
1 chilli, seeded and finely chopped
1 garlic clove, peeled and crushed
2 spring onions, finely chopped
2 tablespoons soy sauce
2 teaspoons sugar
3 tablespoons chicken stock
2 teaspoons cornflour

Preparation time: 5 minutes
Cooking time: 8 minutes

1. Steam the scallops on their shells for 5–6 minutes.
2. Heat the oil in a wok or frying pan and add the black beans, chilli, garlic and spring onions. Stir together, then add the soy sauce, sugar and chicken stock blended with the cornflour. Stir until thickened and pour over the hot scallops on a warmed serving plate. Serve immediately.

STEAMING SCALLOPS

While it is traditional to steam scallops on their shells, it is not necessary to do so. If scallops have been bought without their shells (and many are sold without them today), they may be put on a heatproof plate and cooked in a steamer inside a wok or over a saucepan. If you do not have a steamer, put the plate on a rack in a wok or saucepan containing water and with a good fitting lid. The plate should be a good 5 cm (2 inch) above the water level. It is a good idea to put a strip of foil under the plate so that it can be lifted in and out of the pan.

LEFT, *Ginger and spring onion crab;* RIGHT, *Steamed scallops in black bean sauce*

FISH WRAPPED IN LOTUS LEAVES

1 mullet, sea-bass, carp or trout, about
   1.25 kg (2½ lb)
2 tablespoons soy sauce
1 teaspoon salt
2 tablespoons hoisin sauce
2 tablespoons vegetable oil
2 tablespoons Chinese wine or dry sherry
3 slices root ginger, shredded
3 spring onions, finely chopped
2 lotus leaves

For the stuffing:
1½ tablespoons lard
2 onions, peeled and finely chopped
2 rashers bacon, finely shredded
100 g (4 oz) mushrooms, quartered

Preparation time: 25 minutes, plus
marinating
Cooking time: 50 minutes steaming or 55
minutes baking
Oven: 200°C, 400°F, Gas Mark 6; then
160°C, 325°F, Gas Mark 2

1. Wash and dry the fish. Mix together the soy sauce, salt, hoisin sauce, oil, wine, ginger and spring onion. Rub the fish inside and out with the mixture and leave to marinate for 30 minutes.
2. Heat a wok or frying pan, add the lard and stir until it melts. Add the onions, bacon and mushrooms and stir-fry for 1½ minutes. Remove from the wok and drain on absorbent kitchen paper.
3. Remove the fish from the marinade and stuff with the onion mixture. Wrap carefully in the lotus leaves, then wrap a sheet of foil round to keep the leaves in place.
4. Steam vigorously for 45 minutes, or bake in a preheated oven for 25 minutes, then reduce the heat and bake for another 25 minutes.
5. Serve the fish still wrapped in the lotus leaves, unwrapping it at the table for everyone to help themselves from this pretty and unusual parcel.

CRISPY PRAWN BALLS

4 slices white bread, crusts removed and cut
   into 1 cm (½ inch) cubes
225 g (8 oz) white fish fillets, minced
225 g (8 oz) uncooked prawns, peeled,
   deveined and minced
2 teaspoons salt
pinch of white pepper
2 egg whites, lightly beaten
2 tablespoons cornflour
2 slices root ginger, peeled and finely chopped
600 ml (1 pint) vegetable oil

Preparation time: 20 minutes
Cooking time: 10 minutes

1. Toast the bread cubes lightly until light brown and dry.
2. Mix together the minced fish, prawns, salt, pepper, egg whites, cornflour and finely chopped ginger. Form the mixture into balls, using about 1 tablespoon per ball, then roll each ball in the croutons until coated.
3. Heat the oil in a wok or frying pan to 180°C/350°F or until a cube of bread browns in 30 seconds. Gently lower the balls into the oil and deep-fry until light brown. Remove and drain on absorbent kitchen paper.
4. Serve as an hors d'oeuvre or starter, on a bed of lettuce leaves.

LEFT, Fish wrapped in lotus leaves; RIGHT, Crispy prawn balls

NOODLES AND RICE

Both these foods are staples in Oriental cookery, so not surprisingly, there is plenty of inspiration to be gained from the recipes here. Try the traditional, 'big occasion' dish, Eight Treasure glutinous rice, or, for an unusual way with familiar foods, there are Clay pot chicken rice or Mushroom noodles to whet the appetite.

Yangchow special fried rice (see page 113)

VEGETARIAN CHOW MEIN

SERVES 4–5 as a snack
6 medium Chinese dried mushrooms
450 g (1 lb) Chinese noodles or spaghetti
175 g (6 oz) soy-braised bamboo shoots
   (usually available canned)
4 tablespoons vegetable oil
4 slices root ginger, shredded
2 garlic cloves, peeled and crushed
150 g (5 oz) Chinese cabbage, shredded
75 g (3 oz) Chinese hot Szechuan pickle (Ja-
   Chai), shredded
1 tablespoon Szechuan hot bean sauce (Tou-
   Pan Jeang)
1½ tablespoons hoisin sauce
2 tablespoons light soy sauce
25 g (1 oz) butter
150 g (5 oz) mangetout, finely sliced
150 g (5 oz) bean sprouts
2 spring onions, cut into 2.5 cm (1 inch)
   lengths
1 small red pepper, seeded and shredded
100 g (4 oz) firm button mushrooms, thinly
   sliced
1 teaspoon salt
1 tablespoon dark soy sauce
1 teaspoon sesame oil
1 tablespoon brandy

Preparation time: 25 minutes plus
soaking
Cooking time: 15 minutes (with noodles),
20 minutes (with spaghetti)

An appealing and attractive dish,
of particular interest to vegetarians, of
course, but delicious for everyone!
1. Pour boiling water over the dried
mushrooms to cover. Soak for 30 minutes,
then drain, reserving the mushroom-
soaking water, shred the caps and discard
the stems.
2. Cook the noodles in boiling water for 5
minutes (or the spaghetti for 10 minutes).
Turn off the heat and leave the pasta to
stand in the hot water for 3 minutes or 5
minutes longer respectively. Drain and
rinse in cold water to keep the strands
separate.
3. Cut the soy-braised bamboo shoots into
matchstick shreds.
4. Heat half the oil in a wok or frying pan.
When hot, add the ginger, garlic, dried
mushrooms, shredded cabbage, shredded
pickle and shredded bamboo shoots. Stir-
fry for 2½ minutes over a high heat. Add
the hot bean sauce and hoisin sauce. Stir-
fry for 1 further minute.
5. Turn the noodles or spaghetti into the
pan. Turn and toss them with the
ingredients in the pan, then sprinkle with
soy sauce and half the mushroom water.
Heat through thoroughly, turning a few
times. Remove from the heat.
6. Heat the remaining oil with the butter in
another wok or frying pan. When the
butter has melted, add the mangetout and
stir-fry over a medium heat for 1 minute.
Turn the heat up high and add all the
other vegetables. Sprinkle with the salt
and dark soy sauce, sesame oil and brandy.
Continue to stir and turn the ingredients
in the pan for 1 minute.
7. Transfer the hot noodles to a heated
serving dish Heat the remaining vegetable
mixture for 30 seconds over a high heat.
Pour over the noodles and serve.

CHINESE PICKLES
Numerous pickles are used in Chinese cooking.
Among the most widely used are Winter pickle
(salted cabbage), Snow pickle (salted mustard seeds)
and the hot Szechuan pickle suggested for this recipe.
The last-named is based on kohlrabi and is a
crunchy, yellowish-green pickle with a hot and salty
flavour. Hot Szechuan pickle and Snow pickle are
available in cans and all three can usually be found
in specialist Chinese food stores. They should be
rinsed thoroughly before use.

SINGAPORE NOODLES

2 rounds dry noodles
500 ml (18 fl oz) water
100 g (4 oz) lean pork, cut into 5cm (2 inch)
　strips
75 g (3 oz) uncooked shelled prawns
74 g (3 oz) squid, cleaned and sliced
4 tablespoons vegetable oil
2 garlic cloves, peeled and crushed
75 g (3 oz) beansprouts
1 tablespoon light soy sauce
1 tablespoon dark soy sauce
½ teaspoon pepper
1 bunch fresh chives, chopped
2 eggs

Preparation time: 15 minutes
Cooking time: 17 minutes

The original version of this dish, as sold by Singapore hawkers, is a rich mix of noodles, beansprouts, boiled pork, squid, prawns, egg and rich meat stock. Well-known as a late-night supper dish, it can be modified to suit your taste. Use chicken breast instead of pork, for instance. If squid is not your taste, leave it out. What is important is the stock.

1. Boil the noodles in plenty of water for 2 minutes and drain. Bring the 500 ml (18 fl oz) of water to the boil and cook the pork, prawns and squid for 5 minutes. Drain and reserve the stock.
2. Heat the oil in a wok or frying pan and fry the garlic till light brown. Add the beansprouts and noodles and cook, stirring, for 2 minutes over a high heat.
3. Add the cooked ingredients, sauces, seasoning and chives and stir for another minute.
4. Push to one side of the pan and crack in the eggs. Cook for 1 minute and add the reserved stock. Bring to the boil and cook for 2 minutes, stirring well.
5. Turn the noodles on to a warmed plate and serve at once. Serve sliced chillies and lemon juice in a side dish.

MEE GORENG (CHILLI NOODLES)

150 g (6 oz) dry wheat noodles
4 tablespoons vegetable oil
4 shallots, peeled and sliced
75 g (3 oz) minced lamb
1 teaspoon chilli powder
75 g (3 oz) beansprouts
1 boiled potato, diced
1 tomato, chopped
2 eggs
2 teaspoons salt
1 tablespoon tomato sauce

Preparation time: 10 minutes
Cooking time: 12 minutes

Indian cuisine as found in South-East Asia features this dish prominently but it is totally alien in India. Plagiarized from the Chinese, it took on spicy touches that marry well with the bland staple noodles. It has also become a popular item in Indonesian and Malaysian restaurants because these two cuisines borrow freely from the migrant Indian kitchen.

1. Boil the noodles in plenty of water for 3 minutes and drain.
2. Heat the oil in a wok or frying pan and fry the shallots till light brown.
3. Add the minced lamb, fry for 1 minute, then add the chilli powder, beansprouts, noodles, potato and tomato. Cook, stirring, over a high heat for 2 minutes.
4. Push aside and crack the eggs into the pan. Cook for 1 minute, then cut up with the ladle or stirring spoon. Add the salt and tomato sauce, stir all ingredients back together and cook for another minute. Sprinkle a few drops of water in if the mixture becomes too dry.
5. Tip the mee goreng on to a warmed serving dish and serve at once.

LEFT, Singapore noodles; RIGHT, Mee goreng (chilli noodles)

BEGGAR'S NOODLES

SERVES 4–5 with 1 or 2 other dishes
450 g (1 lb) Chinese noodles or spaghetti
2 tablespoons finely chopped spring onions
1 tablespoon vegetable oil
2½ tablespoons light soy sauce
1 tablespoon brandy

For the sauce:
4 tablespoons peanut butter
2 tablespoons vegetable oil
1 tablespoon sesame oil
1½ teaspoons salt
4 tablespoons chicken stock
1¼ teaspoons red chilli oil or sauce

Preparation time: 10 minutes
Cooking time: 6–12 minutes, plus
standing

An exceptionally simple dish, but one with an excellent, unusual flavour.
1. Cook the noodles in boiling water for 5–6 minutes (or the spaghetti for 10–11 minutes). Turn off the heat, allow the pasta to remain in the hot water for half as long again as the cooking time, then drain. While still hot add the finely chopped spring onions, the vegetable oil, soy sauce and brandy and toss well.
2. Mix all the sauce ingredients in a bowl or jug until thoroughly combined.
3. To serve, pour the sauce evenly over the noodles in individual bowls or one large serving bowl and sprinkle with roughly chopped spring onions.

FUJIAN TWO SHRIMPS NOODLES

SERVES 4–5 as a snack
350 g (12 oz) rice-flour noodles
2 onions, peeled
3 bacon rashers, rinded
75 g (3 oz) Chinese dried shrimps
4 tablespoons vegetable oil
1¾ teaspoons salt
1¾ teaspoons curry powder
5 tablespoons chicken stock
2 tablespoons light soy sauce
25 g (1 oz) butter
3 spring onions, cut into 5 cm (2 inch) lengths
3 garlic cloves, peeled and crushed
200 g (7 oz) fresh or thawed frozen peeled
  prawns
2 tablespoons dry sherry

Preparation time:15 minutes, plus
soaking
Cooking time: about 10 minutes

This is a dish from coastal China. The combination of fresh and dried shrimps is a particularly happy 'marriage'.
1. Soak the noodles in boiling water for 3½ minutes. Drain and rinse under running water to keep the strands separate. Slice the onions thinly and shred the bacon. Soak the dried shrimps in boiling water for 10 minutes then drain.
2. Heat the oil in a wok or frying pan. When hot add the sliced onions, bacon, dried shrimps, ¼ teaspoon salt and curry powder. Stir-fry over medium heat for 3 minutes. Add the stock and mix well.
3. Add the noodles, sprinkle them with soy sauce and stir-fry for 2½ minutes, until thoroughly heated through.

4. Heat the butter in another wok or frying pan. When hot add the spring onions, garlic and the remaining salt. Stir to mix. Add the prawns and sherry and stir-fry over a high heat for 2 minutes.
5. Transfer the noodle mixture to a large, well-heated serving dish. Pour over the prawn mixture and serve immediately.

LEFT, Fujian two shrimps noodles; RIGHT, Beggar's noodles

MUSHROOM NOODLES

500 ml (18 fl oz) water
1 packet instant noodles
1 tablespoon sesame oil
1 tablespoon oyster or HP sauce
1 tablespoon tomato sauce
1 tablespoon chilli sauce (optional)
2 stalks spring onions, chopped
5 or 6 button mushrooms, sliced
2 tablespoons cooked shrimp or ham
1 teaspoon salt
½ teaspoon pepper

Preparation time: 8 minutes
Cooking time: 2 minutes

A great standby dish when you are rushed for time, this tasty one-dish meal can be cooked in minutes if you use ready-to-cook fresh yellow noodles or instant packet noodles that need to be boiled for only 2 minutes and drained. Many people living on their own in fast-paced cities like Singapore and Kuala Lumpur in Malaysia virtually live off this, with variations on the theme as time permits. Only the noodles need to be boiled briefly and the rest is simple assembly. Shrimps, egg, mushrooms, tinned ham, tuna fish and whatever vegetables you have to hand all go to make an appetising meal. Perfect when you don't want to miss a minute of your favourite TV programme.

1. Bring the water to the boil and cook the noodles for 2 minutes. Drain and keep warm.
2. Mix all the other ingredients together in a large bowl and adjust to taste. Add the noodles and toss well. Serve immediately.

LAKSA NOODLES

225 g (8 oz) rice vermicelli
750 ml (1¼ pints) water
150 g (5 oz) beansprouts
225 g (8 oz) chicken breast
½ large onion, peeled and quartered
2 stalks lemon grass
5 candlenuts
2 tablespoons dried shrimp, soaked till soft
1 tablespoon shrimp paste
3 slices galangal
2 teaspoons chilli powder
1 × 400 ml (14 oz) can coconut milk
5 tablespoons vegetable oil
2 tablespoons fish sauce
1 teaspoon sugar
salt
freshly ground black pepper

Preparation time: 30 minutes
Cooking time: 15 minutes

LEFT, Mushroom noodles; RIGHT, Laksa noodles

Truly a glorious invention, a spicy marriage of Indian, Chinese, Indonesian and Thai elements, Laksa is a complete meal in itself. It does take a little time and effort to prepare but the results are well worth it. Its appearance usually coincides with marathon mahjong parties when players sit through an entire weekend clacking the tiles, breaking only to help themselves to yet another bowl of Laksa. This would be cooked in the morning with the sauce kept hot and all the other cooked ingredients in separate dishes at hand to be assembled according to individual taste.

1. Soak the rice vermicelli in boiling water till soft – about 10 minutes.
2. Bring the 750 ml (1¼ pints) water to the boil and scald the beansprouts for 1 minute. Remove them from the water, drain and set aside on a serving dish. Add the chicken breast to the boiling water and cook for 5 minutes. Remove from the water, cool and slice into bite-sized pieces.
3. Grind together in a mortar or blender the onion, lemon grass, candlenuts, shrimp, shrimp paste, galangal and chilli powder.
4. Combine the cooking water and the coconut milk and put in a deep pan.
5. Heat the oil in a wok or frying pan, fry the ground spices for 4 minutes over a medium heat. Transfer to the pan and combine with the coconut milk mixture. Bring to the boil and simmer for 10 minutes. Add the fish sauce and sugar, check the seasoning and adjust to taste.
6. To serve, place a handful each of beansprouts and vermicelli in a soup bowl. Top with a few slices of chicken and pour the hot soup over. For garnishes, use fresh coriander leaves, mint, shredded lettuce or sweet basil leaves. Toppings could include cooked shrimps, squid or scallops, or sliced fish cake.

EIGHT-TREASURE GLUTINOUS RICE

275 g (10 oz) glutinous rice
900 ml (1½ pints) water
3 Chinese mushrooms
1 tablespoon dried shrimps
8 lotus seeds
1 Chinese sausage
3 tablespoons vegetable oil
3 garlic cloves, peeled and crushed
1 tablespoon chopped onion
8 pitted red Chinese dates
1 tablespoon oyster sauce
1 teaspoon salt
1 teaspoon sugar
1 tablespoon sesame oil
½ teaspoon pepper

Preparation time: 45 minutes
Cooking time: 15 minutes

The 'eight treasures' refer to eight ingredients, traditionally cooked with glutinous rice and sometimes stuffed into a deboned duck or goose for roasting (see page 137). In South-East Asian cooking, this has been modified somewhat and is cooked more often as daily fare rather than a festive dish. You don't have to have eight ingredients. Leaving out one or two won't make that much difference to the overall flavour.

1. Wash the rice and leave to soak in the water. Soak the mushrooms in hot water for 15 minutes. Do the same with the dried shrimps. Drain the lotus seeds. Dice the sausage roughly the same size as the lotus seeds. Dice each mushroom into four.

2. Put the rice in a saucepan and cook over a moderate heat for 10 minutes.

3. Meanwhile, heat the oil in a wok or frying pan and fry the garlic and onion for 2 minutes. Add all the other ingredients except the rice and cook, stirring for 2 minutes. By now, the rice should be about done. Transfer the fried ingredients to the rice, cover and cook for 5 minutes.

4. When sufficiently cool, pack firmly into a large bowl and turn out on to a plate to serve the rice as a mound.

GLUTINOUS RICE

Glutinous rice is a relatively short-grained rice, used widely in Oriental cookery. Despite its name, it is completely gluten-free. When it is boiled, it becomes sweet and sticky and is therefore used mainly in baking and confectionery, though it may also be combined with vegetables or chicken for savoury dishes.

Two varieties of glutinous rice are available: black and a more widely used white rice, which has been de-hulled in processing.

MIXED SPICE RICE

2 tablespoons dried shrimps
4 tablespoons oil
6 shallots, sliced
2 green chillies, sliced
3 garlic cloves, peeled and sliced
350 g (12 oz) cold cooked rice
2 eggs
1 tablespoon light soy sauce
½ teaspoon pepper
100 g (4 oz) cooked shrimps
2 stalks spring onions, chopped
2 tablespoons chopped pineapple

Preparation time: 20 minutes
Cooking time: 8 minutes

A richly tangy dish from Indonesia, this is an excellent way of dressing up leftover boiled rice. You stretch it by adding more eggs, meat or whatever.

1. Soak the dried shrimps in a little hot water for 5 minutes. Drain and pound a little.

2. Heat the oil and fry the shallots, chillies, garlic and shrimps for 4 minutes. Add the rice and stir for 1 minute. Push to one side and crack in the eggs. Add the soy sauce and pepper and cook, stirring for 2 minutes. Add the cooked shrimps, spring onions and pineapple and stir for 2 minutes. Adjust seasoning with more soy sauce, if necessary, turn on to a warmed plate and serve hot.

CLAY POT CHICKEN RICE

275 g (10 oz) long-grain rice
600 ml (20 fl oz) water
175 g (6 oz) chicken breast
3 tablespoons lard
2 tablespoons shredded ginger
1 tablespoon sesame oil
1 tablespoon oyster sauce
1 tablespoon dark soy sauce
½ teaspoon pepper
2 stalks spring onions, chopped

Preparation time: 15 minutes
Cooking time: 18 minutes

The utensil referred to here is a rustic clay bowl with one handle, usually with a glazed interior. Chinese are fond of clay pots – they call them 'sand pots' – as they impart a smoky flavour to everything cooked in them. If you get one that is not too large, it can go from the stove straight to the table sizzling with whatever you have cooked.

1. Wash the rice and place it in a pan with the water. Cook over a moderate heat for about 10 minutes until almost dry.

2. Cut the chicken into thin slices.

3. Melt the lard in a clay pot or flame proof casserole over a moderate heat and fry the shredded ginger for 1 minute. Add the remaining ingredients except the rice and stir well, for a minute.

4. Transfer the rice to the clay pot, stir to mix the ingredients well, cover and cook over a low heat for 5 minutes. Allow the rice to settle for 10 minutes before serving.

LEFT, Mixed spice rice; RIGHT, Clay pot chicken rice

YANGCHOW SPECIAL FRIED RICE

5 tablespoons vegetable oil
1 garlic clove, peeled and crushed
3 slices root ginger, shredded
1 onion, peeled and finely chopped
1 red pepper, cored, seeded and sliced
4 dried Chinese mushrooms, soaked for 20
    minutes, drained, stemmed and sliced
¼ cucumber, sliced
50 g (2 oz) peas
4 tomatoes, chopped
75–100 g (3–4 oz) pork, finely cubed
75–100 g (3–4 oz) shrimps
2 teaspoons salt
1 tablespoon winter pickle
450 g (1 lb) cooked long-grain rice
2 tablespoons soy sauce

Preparation time: 20 minutes, plus
soaking
Cooking time: 6–7 minutes

Why Yangchow? Well, Yangchow is a river-port on the lower Yangtze, where fresh water produce are plentiful. It is also a town well-known for its cuisine. Hence Yangchow 'special fried rice' is one stage richer and more elaborate than ordinary fried rice: it should contain pork (or ham), and freshwater shrimps. The pork should be cut into small, half-sugar-lump-size, cubes.

1. Heat the oil in a wok and add the garlic and ginger. Stir-fry for 1 minute then discard the garlic and ginger. Add the vegetables, pork, shrimps, salt and winter pickle and stir-fry over a medium heat for 2–3 minutes. The vegetables should still be crunchy.
2. Add the rice and mix well, on the heat, for 2–3 minutes until heated through.
3. Sprinkle with soy sauce, mix well and serve.

HAINAN CHICKEN RICE

SERVES 4–6
450 g (1 lb) long-grain rice
1 medium-size chicken, about 1.5 kg (3½ lb)
350 g (12 oz) broccoli or fresh spring cabbage
    (greens)
1.5 l (2½ pints) water
1 slice root ginger
2 medium onions, peeled and sliced
3 teaspoons salt
2 chicken stock cubes
100 g (4 oz) green peas

Preparation time: about 30 minutes
Cooking time: 1 hour 25 minutes

LEFT, Yangchow special fried rice; RIGHT, Hainan chicken rice

Hainan is China's southern-most island and is an unsophisticated region which is only lately being developed. It is about the size of Ireland and the one place in China which is distinctly tropical in climate. This is one of its better known dishes.

1. Wash, rinse and boil the rice in an equal amount (volume) of water for 5–6 minutes and leave to stand until cool when the water will have been absorbed into the rice.
2. Chop the chicken through the skin and bone into large, bite-sized pieces; cut the broccoli or greens into similar-sized pieces.
3. Boil the chicken in a large flameproof casserole in the water with the ginger, onion, and salt. When the contents boil, reduce the heat to a simmer and leave to cook gently for 50 minutes.
4. Remove the chicken from the stock and discard the ginger. Skim away some of the excess fat. Add the stock cubes, broccoli (or spring greens) and peas to the stock. Bring to the boil and stir a few times to dissolve the stock cubes.
5. Finally, add the rice to the stock and leave to cook gently for 10–12 minutes until all the stock has been absorbed.
6. Arrange the chicken pieces on top of the rice and vegetables in the casserole, cover and allow the chicken to heat through in 4–5 minutes over the lowest heat.
7. Serve the chicken rice in the casserole, so the diners can help themselves with spoonfuls of the rice and vegetables. The chicken pieces should be eaten by dipping them into dishfuls of a good quality soy sauce to which have been added chopped garlic and spring onion and small amounts of sesame oil to taste.

ORIENTAL SWEETS

Fruit is the subject for several desserts here, used in tartlets, fritters, a punch and in that famous restaurant treat, Peking toffee apples.
But you will also find tapioca, lotus seeds, rice and bean paste, all used to make delicious and unusual endings for meals.

Kueh bankek (see page 122)

RICE-STUFFED PEARS

225 g (8 oz) flaked rice
25 g (1 oz) almonds, skinned and roughly
    chopped
1 × 100 g (4 oz) can lotus seeds, drained and
    roughly chopped
6 red and green glace cherries, finely chopped
50 ml (2 fl oz) vegetable oil
2 tablespoons sugar
4 pears, peeled, halved and cored

For the sauce:
1 tablespoon sugar
100 ml (3½ fl oz) water
25 g (1 oz) cornflour
1-2 drops pink food colouring (optional)

Preparation time: 10 minutes
Cooking time: 40 minutes

These pears may be cored and halved and the 'stuffing' used to cover them, or they may be cored and left whole, the rice stuffing being pushed down the core. The cooking time would take a few minutes longer.
1. Cover the flaked rice with water and steam for 30 minutes.
2. Mix together the cooked rice, almonds, lotus seeds, cherries, vegetable oil and sugar.
3. To make the sauce, dissolve the sugar in the water. Blend the cornflour with the food colouring (if using) and add this to the sugar and water. Bring to the boil to form a sauce.
4. Stuff the rice mixture into the pear halves. Place the stuffed pear halves in a steamer basket and steam for about 15 minutes.
5. Serve the stuffed pears with the sauce poured over.

PEKING TOFFEE APPLES

100 g (4 oz) plain flour
1 egg
100 ml (3½ fl oz) water, plus 2 tablespoons
4 crisp apples, peeled, cored and cut into 12
    wedges
600 ml (1 pint) vegetable oil, plus 1
    tablespoon
6 tablespoons sugar
2 tablespoons water
3 tablespoons golden syrup

Preparation time: 15 minutes
Cooking time: 20 minutes

1. Mix together the flour, egg and 100ml (3½ fl oz) of the water to make a batter. Dip each piece of apple into the batter.
2. In a wok or deep frying pan heat 600 ml (1 pint) of the oil to 180°C/350°F or until a cube of bread browns in 30 seconds. Deep-fry the apple pieces for 2 minutes, then remove and drain on absorbent kitchen paper.
3. In another pan, heat together the sugar, and the remaining vegetable oil and water. Dissolve the sugar over a gentle heat, then simmer for 5 minutes, stirring constantly. Add the golden syrup and boil until the hard crack stage is reached (151°C/304°F) or until it forms brittle threads when dropped into iced water. Put in the fried apples and turn to coat each piece.
4. Remove the apple pieces with a slotted spoon and drop into iced water. Remove immediately and serve.

LEFT, Rice-Stuffed pears; RIGHT, Peking toffee apples

STICKY RICE CAKES

MAKES about 14
225 g (8 oz) flaked rice
100 g (4 oz) plain flour
5 tablespoons red bean paste
150 ml (¼ pint) vegetable oil
2 tablespoons sugar

Preparation time: 15 minutes
Cooking time: 35–40 minutes

1. Place the flaked rice in a bowl with enough water to cover, place in a steamer and steam for about 30 minutes.
2. Remove the rice from the steamer, turn out and mix with the plain flour. Knead together to form a dough. Divide into about 14 even-sized pieces. Roll these into balls and then flatten them with the palm of your hand. Put about 2 teaspoons of red bean paste in the centre of the dough and then bring up the sides to completely enclose the red bean paste. Flatten again to about 2.5 cm (1 inch) thick.
3. Heat the oil in a wok to 180°C/350°F, or until a cube of bread browns in 30 seconds and then put the rice cakes into the oil. Fry gently for 3 minutes on each side or until golden brown, then lift out and drain on absorbent kitchen paper. Transfer to a serving plate, sprinkle with sugar and serve immediately.

RED BEAN PASTE

Red bean paste, also called sweet soy bean paste or sauce, is a thick, sweet, red-coloured paste, sold in cans. It is usually available from specialist Chinese food stores. It can be used as a dip, or brushed on to pancakes served with Peking Duck, or made the base of sweet sauces and puddings or confectionery. It is also good served with savoury crispy dishes, like prawn cutlets or quick-roast pork.

MERINGUE BALLS WITH BEAN PASTE STUFFING

1 × 225 g (8 oz) can red bean paste
6 egg whites
pinch of cornflour
100 g (4 oz) plain flour, plus extra for dusting
300 ml (½ pint) vegetable oil
2 tablespoons sugar

Preparation time: 15 minutes
Cooking time: about 3–4 minutes

1. Make 20 small balls with the red bean paste, using about 2 teaspoons of paste for each ball.
2. Beat the egg whites to form stiff peaks. Fold in the pinch of cornflour and plain flour.
3. Dust the prepared bean paste balls with plain flour, then coat well with beaten egg white.
4. Heat the vegetable oil in a wok or frying pan, then put in the coated red bean paste balls and fry gently until golden brown and puffed up. Drain on absorbent kitchen paper and sprinkle with sugar. Transfer to a warmed plate and serve immediately.

CLOKWISE FROM TOP RIGHT, Sticky rice cakes; Meringue balls with bean paste stuffing, Tropical fruit punch (see page 124)

PETITE PINEAPPLES

MAKES about 40
450 g (1 lb) plain flour
2 teaspoons baking powder
300 g (11 oz) chilled butter
2 tablespoons caster sugar
3 egg yolks
½ teaspoon vanilla essence
pinch of salt
2 drops yellow food colouring
120 ml (4 fl oz) boiling water
6 small pineapples
500 g (1¼ lb) granulated sugar
7.5 cm (3 inch) stick cinnamon
whole cloves
1 egg lightly beaten

Preparation time: 1½ hours, plus chilling
Cooking time: 1 hour
Oven: 160°C, 325°F, Gas Mark 3

One of the few sweet items in South-East Asian cuisine that uses butter, this delicious Chinese New Year tidbit is derived from Eurasian influences. You can also make them as open tartlets. If it is not the season for those very small pineapples from Singapore which come into the shops about Christmas time, use one average-size pineapple instead.

1. Sift the flour and baking powder into a mixing bowl. Rub the butter in with the fingertips till the mixture resembles coarse breadcrumbs.
2. Beat the caster sugar, egg yolks, vanilla essence, salt and food colouring lightly till well blended. Pour into a mixing bowl with the boiling water and knead well to form a pastry dough. Chill for an hour.
3. Remove the skin and core from the pineapples and chop the flesh till very fine. Drain (but do not squeeze) in a fine mesh seive. Cook the pineapple, granulated sugar and cinnamon over a moderate heat, stirring constantly, until almost dry and jam-like. Discard the cinnamon stick and chill.
4. Roll out the pastry on a floured board and knead for a few minutes. Divide into several portions for easier handling.
5. Roll out each piece to 5 mm (¼ inch) thick. Cut out circles each about 5 cm (2 inch) across. Place a teaspoon of pineapple jam on each piece, and fold up into a small egg shape (a pigeon's egg, in fact).
6. Remove the bud from a clove and stick it into the broader end of the 'egg'. Use a small pair of scissors to make V-shaped snips all around to resemble a pineapple.
7. Place the finished tarts on lightly greased trays. Glaze with beaten egg and bake in a preheated moderate oven for 25 minutes.
8. Cool the tarts on a wire tray.

BANANA FRITTERS

4 ripe bananas, skinned
3 tablespoons plain flour
2 tablespoons self-raising flour
½ teaspoon salt
85 ml (3 fl oz) water
1 egg, beaten
600 ml (20 fl oz) oil for deep-frying
vanilla ice cream
golden syrup

Preparation time: 10 minutes
Cooking time: 10 minutes

LEFT, Petite pineapples; RIGHT, Banana fritters

This tropical snack has been further hybridised in London restaurants serving Malaysian and Indonesian cuisine. They add a scoop or two of vanilla ice cream to the hot fritters and top it all off with golden syrup. Strange at first taste, but the contrasts of flavours and hot and cold are absolutely delicious.

1. Slice each banana into two diagonally. Sift the flours and salt into a bowl and mix with the water to a smooth batter. Blend the egg well.
2. Heat the oil to 180°C/350°F, or until a cube of bread browns in 30 seconds. Dip each piece of banana into the batter, drip any excess batter off and deep-fry in hot oil till golden brown.

3. Serve the Banana fritters hot with a scoop of vanilla ice cream and golden syrup spooned over.

KUEH BANKEK

225 g (8 oz) rice flour
225 g (8 oz) tapioca flour
2 large eggs
150 g (5 oz) sugar
½ teaspoon salt
150 ml (5 fl oz) thick coconut milk

Preparation time: 30 minutes plus cooling
Cooking time: 45 minutes
Oven: 180°C, 350°F, Gas Mark 4

These are extremely easy to make and children will love them. More like biscuits than a pudding, they belong to the 'cakes to clean your palate with' range. Stored in an air-tight cookie jar, they keep for months. Flours used for making these and other sweetmeats are traditionally dried in the sun for days or dry-fried till very 'light'.

1. In a dry non-stick pan or wok, fry the flours separately on a low heat till very light. Cool the flours completely, then combine them and sift into a mixing bowl.
2. Beat the eggs, sugar, salt and coconut milk together till creamy and thick.
3. Pour into the mixing bowl with the flours and make a firm dough by kneading the mixture for a few minutes.

4. Roll out the dough on a floured board to 5 mm (¼ inch) thickness. Cut out different shapes with cookie cutters and roll out again, going through the whole process, till the dough is used up.
5. Bake on a greased tray in a preheated oven for 25 minutes. The biscuits should be a pale bleached colour. Cool on a wire tray.

ALMOND FLOAT

300 ml (½ pint) cold water
2 packets unflavoured gelatine
300 ml (½ pint) milk
1 tablespoon almond extract
*1 × 185 g (6½ oz) can manderin orange
    segments*

Syrup:
100 g (4 oz) sugar
500 ml (18 fl oz) cold water

Preparation time: 5 minutes, plus setting
Cooking time: 15 minutes

This cool and delicate looking pudding, which could provide a light finish to just about any menu, comes from China's great eastern plain round the Yangtse delta, just north of Shanghai.

1. In a large bowl, mix together 100 ml (3½ fl oz) of cold water and the gelatine and let it soften for about 5 minutes. Bring the remaining water to the boil in a small pan and then add the gelatine mixture. Stir over heat until it becomes clear, then stir in the milk and almond extract. Pour it all into a shallow dish and leave it to set in a cool place.
2. Meanwhile, make the syrup: combine the sugar and water in a small pan and

bringing it to the boil. Stir and mix well. Cool in the refrigerator. This sauce will be thin.
3. When set, cut the almond jelly into squares or diamond shapes and arrange on a dish. Decorate with the mandarin segments and pour the syrup over.

CLOCKWISE FROM LEFT, Kueh bankek; Lotus seed pudding (see page 124); Almond float

LOTUS SEED PUDDING

200 g (7 oz) sugar
750 ml (1¼ pints) water, plus 3 tablespoons
1½ tablespoons arrowroot
1 × 400 g (14 oz) can cooked lotus seeds

Preparation time: 15 minutes
Cooking time: 20 minutes

Illustrated on page 123

This is eaten by the Chinese more for symbolism than anything else, though it is delicious. To eat lotus seeds means to have more progeny, the more hands to till the farm with.

1. In a dry pot, caramelize the sugar over a low heat till golden brown. Add 750ml (1¼ pints) of the water and bring to the boil.

2. Dissolve the arrowroot in the remaining water and stir in to the sugar syrup to thicken slowly. Cook until 'gooey' and add the lotus seeds in the last few minutes. Cool and chill if you want to serve it cold. It is just as delicious hot.

TROPICAL FRUIT PUNCH

SERVES 2
1 fresh coconut
½ honeydew melon
1 × 400 g (14 oz) can pineapples, liquidized
crushed ice
dash of rum
pinch of cinnamon

Preparation time: 15 minutes

Illustrated on page 119

Although called a 'punch', this delicious concoction is really a dessert, since it is much too thick to drink: you will need a spoon to scoop it up.

1. Split the coconut into two with a sharp cleaver, and scoop out the soft meat. Wash, dry and set aside the coconut halves.

2. Cut the honeydew melon in half, scoop out the flesh and cut into fine dice. Combine with the coconut meat and pineapple juice and pour over crushed ice in glass dessert dishes or the coconut halves. Add a dash of rum to each and a pinch of cinnamon.

FOOD FACTS

HELEN DORE

CHINESE CUISINE

Cooking plays an important part in the history of civilization, so it is not surprising that the Chinese, with their outstanding cultural tradition reaching back thousands of years, have a fascinating culinary history as well. In fact, their cuisine has changed remarkably little over the centuries, with classic treasured recipes handed down from generation to generation. In China the sense of family is very strong: the Chinese have a deep love of children and respect for the elderly, and in many Chinese restaurants it is common to see several generations of one family gathered round the table sharing a meal together.

The continuity of the Chinese culinary tradition has extended far beyond the frontiers of China itself. With so many Chinese living abroad, many major cities, like London, Bombay, New York and San Francisco, have their own 'Chinatown', with restaurants, shops and everything that expresses the Chinese way of life. A visit to Chinatown is a fascinating experience in any part of the world – a wonderful opportunity to sample Chinese food at its best and most authentic, to explore the shelves of the grocery stores and supermarkets and discover the intriguing ingredients which give oriental cooking its special flavour. You will find details of many of these on pages 130–1, while several more are described in hint boxes by specific recipes throughout the book.

Many Western supermarkets, too, cater increasingly for the tremendous interest that exists in Chinese food, and anyone wishing to cook a Chinese meal at home will be able to find many of the basic ingredients, particularly oils and sauces and an increasing number of Oriental vegetables and fruits, in a local

supermarket. Fortunately Chinese cooking is no longer regarded as mysterious and impenetrable as it was in the past. The basic techniques, of which the most widely used are stir-frying and steaming, are really very simple, and you will find full descriptions of them, together with information on preparation and the equipment required to cook in the Chinese style, on pages 132–7.

Another reason for the increasing popularity of Chinese cuisine in the West is not only that it is delicious, appetizing in its visual appeal as well as its taste, but extremely healthy as well. One of the basics of ancient Chinese philosophy, which continues to colour the Chinese outlook on life today, is an emphasis on the importance of harmony and a sense of balanced contrasts in all things. This is reflected in Chinese cooking as well, resulting in an ideally balanced, wholesome and nutritious diet, with a strong emphasis on natural ingredients – fresh vegetables in great variety, lean meat, low-fat chicken, fish and seafood, eggs and rice. Because the food is usually cooked quickly, all its natural goodness, colour and texture are retained.

Chinese cuisine is also very versatile, flexible and adaptable, so perfect for modern cooks. Flavour variations can easily be achieved by interchanging ingredients, and the Chinese diet can be ideal for vegetarians, offering a tremendous variety of dishes without meat. It can also be highly economical, for example using small quantities of meat or fish in combination with plenty of less expensive fresh vegetables and rice.

The Chinese are very sociable, hospitable people, with a strong sense of community and togetherness: this can be seen in the way they serve a meal from a variety of dishes set in the centre of a round table so that everybody can join in, helping themselves and fellow diners to the food. So Chinese cooking is ideal for home entertaining, and on pages 140–1 you will find ideas for serving a Chinese meal in authentic style, to create a social occasion with a difference.

The great size of China makes it inevitable that cooking styles should differ from one part of the country to another. In fact, China may be divided into four distinct culinary regions: the North, Canton, Szechuan and Eastern China.

The recipes in this book come from a wide spread of the Oriental world. This map, centred on China and South-East Asia, indicates the main areas of the cuisines included, plus the many neighbouring countries whose cooking has influenced, and been influenced by, those cuisines.

USSR

MONGOLIA

NORTH KOREA

JAPAN

SOUTH KOREA

Great Wall

● Peking
(Beijing)

SHANTUNG

C H I N A

Hwang Ho

KIANGSU

HONAN

● Yangchow

Nanking ●

● Shanghai

PAKISTAN

SZECHUAN

Chengtu ●

Yangtze

FUKIEN

KWANGTUNG

TAIWAN

NEPAL

TIBET

Canton ●

BANGLADESH

Si Kiang

HONG KONG

INDIA

BURMA

LAOS

HAINAN ISLAND

THAILAND

VIETNAM

P
H
I
L
I
P
P
I
N
E
S

Bangkok ●

CAMBODIA

BRUNEI

M A L A Y S I A

● SINGAPORE

I N D O N E S I A

THE NORTH

The northernmost frontier of China is marked by the Great Wall, and beyond this lie the great steppes of Mongolia and Central Asia. Mutton and lamb were brought to northern China by the Mongols in the 13th and 14th centuries, and have remained popular there ever since, although they are rarely eaten elsewhere in China. Another distinguishing characteristic of the northern region is its vast grasslands: wheat flour features widely in north Chinese cooking, to make noodles, buns, dumplings and pancakes.

Peking (Beijing), the ancient capital of China, has a light and elegant cuisine, with crisply roasted Peking Duck, eaten wrapped in wafer-thin pancakes, as its most famous speciality. The province of Honan, on the Hwang Ho (Yellow) river, is famous for its sweet and sour specialities and for its freshwater fish, especially carp. Shantung, with its extensive coast-line, has an abundance of shellfish.

CANTON

This south-eastern region is renowned for the excellence and variety of its cuisine, drawing on a wealth of natural ingredients: fresh vegetables, meat – especially pork, poultry, fish and seafood. The semi-tropical climate produces delicious fruit, especially citrus – tangerines, mandarin oranges, grapefruit and loquats. The Cantonese are famous for their *dim sum*, delicious savoury snack food served at tea houses during the afternoon. The first Chinese to emigrate in large numbers in the 19th century were from Canton, and it is Cantonese cuisine that has contributed so much to the popularity of Chinese cooking abroad.

SOUTH-EAST ASIAN CUISINE

The area collectively described here as South-East Asia consists of Thailand, the Malay Peninsula and the islands of Indonesia. The whole region is one great melting-pot, with an influx throughout history of traders, entrepreneurs and fortune-hunters from India, Ceylon (Sri Lanka), Goa and the Arab countries, Portuguese and Dutch merchants, British settlers, and successive waves of immigrants from China, who settled primarily in Malacca and became known as Straits Chinese to distinguish them from Mainland Chinese.

South-East Asian cuisine is as exciting and varied as the people themselves, a fascinating mix of pure ethnic and hybrid recipes, with particularly strong influences from India (three centuries ago the region was part of a thriving Hindu empire) and neighbouring China. Today a Singapore family is quite likely to sit down to a meal of Cantonese soup, Malay curry, a Western salad and an Indian dessert, showing just how cosmopolitan the cooking is. In recent years Indonesian and Thai cuisine has become increasingly familiar and popular in the West, with a number of restaurants of both nationalities opening in London and other cities.

In South-East Asia the tropical climate results in particularly lush vegetation. Vegetables and herbs, especially lemon grass, coriander, chives, curry and turmeric leaves, grow in great profusion and variety, as a visit to one of the many colourful open markets reveals. Here you will find yams, okra, green and purple aubergines, pumpkin and marrows, Chinese cabbage and mustard greens, chillis, sweet potatoes, beansprouts and bamboo shoots, water chestnuts and all kinds of salad leaves. Vegetables are a fundamental part of the South-East Asian diet and vegetable dishes of all kinds are specially prized: raw salads like the tremendously popular *gado gado*, served with a spicy sauce; braised vegetables; deep-fried vegetable fritters; mixed vegetable stir-fries, curries, biryanis, pickles, relishes and side dishes.

Fruit is wonderful too, of course, especially pineapple, mangoes, pawpaw, melons, lychees, star-fruit and many varieties of banana. Fruit is often mixed with vegetables in salads, as in the Tropical Great Salad on page 34. Fruit and meat is also a popular combination, as in Stir-fried Beef and Pineapple on page 43. Lemons and limes are widely used in savoury dishes, especially with fish and poultry.

Nuts are another special feature of South-East Asian cuisine. Coconut milk, extracted from the grated fibrous coconut flesh, is an important ingredient in many dishes (see Coconut Grilled Chicken on page 71). Coconut oil, obtained by boiling

SZECHUAN

This great mountain-ringed basin lying in western China has a rich fertile soil and mild climate. Hot, spicy food is characteristic of the region. Spices – especially peppercorns – herbs and fiery red chilli peppers are used liberally in Szechuan cuisine. A variety of ways of preserving food – salting, drying, smoking and pickling – is also characteristic of the Szechuan art of cooking. Szechuan hot pickle is a popular ingredient, and chillis are used in all sorts of ways, to spice food and also to flavour the oil in which it is cooked. (The chillis may be removed from the oil before the food is added, to give a milder flavour.)

EASTERN CHINA

The delta of the mighty Yangtze river, an amazing 3,000 miles long from its source in the Plateau of Tibet, is one of the most fertile areas on earth. Crops include wheat, rice, barley, sweet potatoes, peanuts and soy beans. Freshwater and deep-sea fish abound. Huaiyang cuisine,

based on Yangchow in the Yangtze delta, is famous for dumplings and noodles – in fact it is probable that pasta was first introduced to Italy from this fertile region by Marco Polo, on his return from China in the 14th century.

Shanghai, with its colourful cosmopolitan history as one of the great trading centres of the east, has a rich, sophisticated, varied cuisine, featuring many gastronomic delights from all over China. In marked contrast is the cuisine of Fukien province in the south, with its accent on locally produced delicacies, especially seafood and agricultural products.

---

down coconut milk, is used to fry the spice mixtures which are so characteristic of South-East Asian cooking. There are many variations, too, on the spicy peanut sauce which is the traditional dipping accompaniment to satay skewers, one of Indonesia's best-known and most delicious national dishes.

Fish have always been important in South-East Asia, with its long mainland coastline and myriad islands. Some of the finest dishes of the region are based on seafood and fish, which abound in the sea, rivers and inland freshwater ponds and paddy fields. Huge juicy prawns, oysters, scallops, clams, abalone, lobsters and crabs are common along with snapper, whitebait, catfish, mackerel, bass and squid, to name just a few of the innumerable varieties. There are just as many delicious ways of cooking fish and seafood, too: steamed, wrapped in fragrant banana leaves, grilled in satay,

spiced in mild curries or fiery hot *samblas*, served in a sweet and sour sauce or made into soup.

Meats such as beef and pork are usually supplemented with lots of vegetables, beancurd or noodles in main course recipes. Buddhists and Hindus, who represent a large section of the population, will not eat beef, nor Muslims pork, on religious grounds, which is perhaps one of the reasons why poultry – always free-range, of course – is so popular in South-East Asia. There are hundreds of recipes for cooking chicken: braised, curried, grilled, stir-fried, stewed and sweet and sour chicken dishes all feature in this book, as well as a delicious spicy chicken soup on page 14.

Noodles are often the basis of main course recipes, either served in a tamarind or coconut gravy, or crisp-fried, with vegetables, meat and seafood. The Singapore Noodles and Laksa Noodles

recipes in this book (pages 102 and 107) show just how substantial main-course noodle dishes can be. Nasi goreng, a delicious main-course noodle dish, is probably one of the best-known South-East Asian dishes in the West, along with gado gado. Noodles are also eaten as very popular snacks at any time of day, sold from roadside stalls.

Rice is a staple ingredient here, as in many Asian countries, where it is a large part of many people's daily diet and is regarded with reverence: according to Chinese tradition it is bad luck ever to let your rice bin become empty. In South-East Asia starchy glutinous rice and fragrant Thai rice are among the most popular types, but there are endless variations on the theme of cooking rice – steamed, plain-boiled, fried with eggs, vegetables, meat or seafood, flavoured with saffron, in pilaus, stuffings and fillings for savoury vegetable leaf packages.

ORIENTAL COOKING INGREDIENTS

The ingredients described here occur frequently in Oriental recipes. They are available in this country in Chinese food stores. An increasing number of them may also be bought in some supermarkets.

Bamboo shoots: the white inner part of the young bamboo plant is sold fresh in Far Eastern markets, when it must be peeled and boiled before use in cooking, but it is most widely available canned in the West. Drained canned bamboo shoots lend crispness and texture to stir-fried dishes.

Bean curd: also known as *tofu*, this almost tasteless product of puréed yellow soy beans is very high in protein, and is available from health food shops as well as Chinese grocers. Ordinary beancurd is sold in blocks; silken beancurd, which is much softer, is sold in vacuum-packed containers. Dried beancurd is sold in cake form and can be cut into strips or slices and stewed, braised or fried. Although naturally very bland in flavour, beancurd benefits from being cooked with spicy sauces, and is specially good as a vegetarian source of protein. It blends well with vegetables in stir-fries.

Beansprouts: these are the sprouts of small green mung beans, which are available fresh and canned, and can also be easily grown at home – they will sprout within a few days. Very inexpensive, with no preparation required, beansprouts are often included in crunchy Chinese vegetable mixtures. They should be cooked only very briefly, to retain maximum crispness. Stored in a polythene bag, tightly sealed, and kept in the vegetable drawer of the refrigerator, they will keep fresh for several days.

Black beans: salted or fermented, these are available in polythene bags and cans from Chinese food stores. They need to be pre-soaked for 5–10 minutes in cold water,

before adding to meat or seafood.

Black bean paste: often used instead of soy sauce in stir-frying, when a thicker, less liquid sauce is required. It, too, is readily available from Chinese food stores.

Candlenuts: also known as kemiri nuts (*buah keras* in Malay), these creamy white nuts, the shape and size of macadamia nuts, are not edible raw but are widely used in South-East Asian cooking as a thickener and sweetener. They can be bought in Chinese food stores and will keep indefinitely in the refrigerator.

Chilli paste: made from chillis, soy beans, salt, sugar and flour. Sold in jars.

Chilli sauce: this hot-tasting sauce made from red chilli peppers is extensively used in Szechuan cuisine.

Coconut milk: an indispensable ingredient in many South-East Asian dishes, this is obtained from grating fresh coconut flesh. In Malaysia, there are special stalls for shelling, grating and squeezing coconut for this purpose. In the West, it is more practicable to use coconut cream in blocks, which is reconstituted by adding boiling water, or to buy canned coconut milk from Chinese food stores. Coconut milk powder, which is simply mixed with water, is also available.

Five-spice powder: star anise, Szechuan peppercorns, fennel, cloves and cinnamon are mixed together and ground to a cocoa-coloured powder which is very pungent

and needs to be used sparingly to season meat and poultry.

Galangal: also known as Laos Root, this is a member of the ginger family but has a stronger flavour than ginger itself, so should be used only in recipes that call for it and not as a substitute for ginger.

Ginger root: very widely used as a flavouring in Oriental cuisine, particularly with fish, seafood and strong-tasting meat such as beef. It should be peeled and finely sliced or chopped before use. Ginger juice may be extracted from the root by placing the small peeled slices in a garlic crusher and squeezing firmly. Ginger root is available fresh, dried and pickled, and is usually sold by weight.

Hoisin sauce: a thick, soy-based sauce with a sweet, hot flavour and a reddish-brown colour. Used with soy sauce in stir-frying, or for cooking spareribs, and may also be served as a dip.

Lemon grass: this sub-tropical plant with a small white bulb and pale green leaves about 25 cm (10 inch) long lends a wonderful, pungent lemon flavour to South-East Asian dishes, especially seafood and chicken. The bulb may be ground in spice mixtures; the leaves may be bruised or sliced and cooked in sauces, or used as an aromatic garnish.

Lime leaves: the edible, fragrant, glossy dark green leaves of a lime tree indigenous to South-East Asia are wonderful shredded in Indonesian curried dishes. Stored in a tightly sealed polythene bag they will keep for up to 3 weeks in the refrigerator, or for several months in the freezer.

Lotus root: has a distinctive pattern when sliced, and is available canned or dried in the West. Dried lotus root should be soaked in water overnight before use in mixed vegetable dishes.

Lotus seeds: also sold dried and canned, are oval and about 1 cm (½ inch) long. They are used in braised vegetable dishes, soups and savoury stuffings. Sugared lotus seeds are eaten as a festival sweet.

Lotus leaves: sold dried in packages in Chinese food stores, used for wrapping foods to be steamed.

Macadamia nuts: indispensable thickening agents in Malaysian curry pastes, ground or pounded with curry spices.

Mushrooms: Chinese dried mushrooms, which need soaking for 20 minutes in warm water before use, give a delicious flavour to soups, stuffings and meat dishes. Wood ears (also known as cloud-ears), are a tree fungus, greyish-black in colour; they lend a crunchy texture to vegetable mixtures and stir-fries.

Noodles: made from hard wheat flour, as in Italian pasta, and water or eggs, are available round or flat, in a variety of widths, fresh from Chinese food stores, or – more widely available – in dried form. Fresh noodles take only 5–8 minutes to cook in boiling water, dried take longer – about 10–15 minutes. They are then drained and added to soups and stir-fries.

Rice noodles are white and thread-like and are available round or flat in packets from Chinese food stores. They are especially good with seafood.

Cellophane noodles, also called beanthread noodles, are a by-product of the mung bean. They are transparent and need to be soaked in water for 5 minutes before use.

Oyster sauce: a very tasty combination of soy sauce and oysters, used mainly in the south of China.

Palm sugar: a brown-coloured, moist sweetener derived from palm, usually sold in plastic packs and available from specialist Chinese food stores.

Pickles: winter pickle, made from salted cabbage, is greenish in colour, with a savoury, mildly salty flavour and comes in jars. Snow pickle, made from salted mustard greens, is greenish in colour with a salty, slightly sour flavour, and is available canned. Szechuan hot pickle is based on kohlrabi and is crunchy, yellowish-green in colour, hot and salty. It is also available in cans. All Chinese pickles should be rinsed thoroughly before being cooked with meat and vegetables.

Rice wine: made from glutinous round-grained rice, with a golden amber colour, is used as a flavouring ingredient and may be replaced with dry sherry if unavailable.

Sesame oil: made from sesame seeds, has a strong, nutty flavour and is used for seasoning rather than cooking. A few drops may be added to soups or prawns fried in batter.

Shrimp paste: also known as *blachan* in Malay, is a very pungent concentrate of dried shrimps, indispensable to curries, sambals and other savoury dishes. As it is so strong-smelling it is best kept wrapped in foil, well away from other foods. It is usually sold in sealed plastic bags.

Soy sauce: made from soy beans, is salty and should be used with caution in cooking. Light soy sauce has a more delicate flavour than dark soy sauce which imparts a rich colour to food. In cooking, soy sauce is best used in conjunction with other ingredients such as wine and stock. It may also be used as a condiment, to season cooked foods lightly, or as a dip, in combination with other sauces, vinegar, sugar, onion, garlic, ginger, etc.

Spring roll skin: made from bean curd (and not to be confused with the Spring rolls on most Chinese restaurant menus!), these thin sheets are cut into strips and used to wrap round a savoury filling of pork, shrimps, chopped water chestnuts, etc. which are then deep– or shallow-fried and served with a tasty dipping sauce.

Szechuan peppercorns: native to Szechuan, are reddish-brown, and much more aromatic than ordinary peppercorns.

Star anise: a dried, star-shaped seed head with a pungent, aromatic flavour like that of fennel seeds. One of the ingredients of five-spice powder.

Tamarind: the dried fruit of the tamarind tree lends a distinctive astringent flavour to Indonesian curries. Both the seed pods and dried pulp of the fruit are used, and may be replaced with lemon or lime juice if unavailable.

ORIENTAL COOKING TECHNIQUES

Chinese cooking techniques are very much methods of heat control (called *he hou*). Although some 40 or 50 such methods are used in China, we need to know only a few of them, particularly stir-frying, deep and shallow frying, steaming, braising and roasting.

South-east Asian culinary techniques depend very much on the open charcoal stove for cooking, since Western-style ovens and grills are little known. The Chinese wok is widely used.

STIR-FRYING

This is one of the most popular cooking methods in China and South-East Asia. The food is cooked quickly over intense heat in a wok (see page 134) in oil, with seasonings and optional stock, wine and sauces. The beauty of stir-frying is that a great variety of foods can be cooked this way – meat, offal, poultry, seafood, vegetables, rice, noodles, and so on – either singly or in combination, to make a complete 'one-pot' in a very short time.

Although the wok is the ideal utensil for stir-frying, it does not always balance readily on modern gas-cooker rings, and a large, thin-bottomed sauce pan or frying pan may be used instead.

Once you have mastered the art of stir-frying, you will find that it offers endless variations on the same basic theme. Here are some ideas for foods that respond specially well to the stir-fry treatment:
chicken breast
beef steak
pork fillet
offal, especially liver and kidney
prawns
squid
mangetout
beansprouts
bamboo shoots
carrot sticks
shredded leeks
sliced courgettes
sliced runner beans
shelled broad beans
mushrooms
shredded cabbage, spring greens or
    Chinese leaves
sliced or diced sweet pepper
sliced or chopped spring onion
lightly cooked noodles
broccoli florets

To stir-fry with success it is important to remember the following basic tips:
■ Cut the food into pieces of similar shape and size, so that it cooks evenly. It may be thinly sliced, shredded or diced, depending on the ingredients used.
■ The wok must be pre-heated before the cooking oil is added.
■ Choose a good-quality cooking oil: groundnut or sunflower would be suitable, as they are light and not too flavoured.
■ Heat the oil (about 2 tablespoons) until smoking, then allow to cool slightly until sizzling before adding the food.
■ For extra flavour, fry seasonings like garlic, ginger, chilli pepper or a ground spice mixture in the oil before starting to stir-fry.
■ Keep the heat high, to ensure brief cooking time.
■ Ingredients requiring longer cooking should be added first.
■ Stir the food vigorously and continuously with chopsticks or a spatula, keeping it on the move all the time as it cooks.

■ Cook the food until just tender but still crisp, with attractive texture and colour. Timing is crucial in stir-frying but it is difficult to specify exact cooking times in recipes as these will depend on the nature of the ingredients and the sizes into which the pieces of food have been cut. As a rule, stir-frying takes only a few minutes if the heat is as high as it should be. At all costs avoid overcooking as this will give soggy, unattractive looking and unappetizing results.
■ Brisk cooking over high heat releases the juices from the food to make a natural gravy, but stock, rice wine or sherry, hoisin sauce, etc. may be added if a richer sauce is required. Make sure, however, that the shape and colour of the ingredients will be shown to best advantage in the stock or sauce you are adding.
■ Stir-fried food should be served immediately it is ready – either straight from the wok, for which special stands are available so that it will sit steadily on a flat surface, or in a pre-heated serving dish.

STEAMING

This is another favourite Chinese cooking method, highly recommended as it is a very healthy way of cooking, requiring no oil or fat, with no loss of valuable nutrients, and keeping food deliciously moist and succulent.

The food to be steamed is placed in a perforated container, then set over boiling water in a large pan. Steaming can be very successfully done in a wok, proving just how versatile this piece of Chinese cooking equipment is, or of course in an ordinary saucepan. It is essential that at no stage should the food come into contact with the water – bear this in mind especially if you are topping up the water level during long steaming.

The Chinese use attractive bamboo steamers, which can be conveniently stacked on top of each other, so that a number of dishes can be steamed simultaneously. Food requiring longest

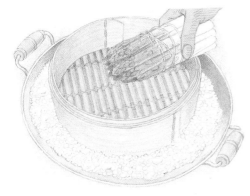

cooking should be placed at the bottom of the stack. Or an expandable stainless steel steamer may be used – handy because it will fit any size of pan and takes up minimal storage space. You could also improvise successfully with a metal colander, or a heatproof plate set on a rack.

Quick steaming is done in an open steamer. The cooking time is brief, and this style of steaming is particularly suitable for tender vegetables and small whole fish or fillets of large fish. Fish cooked like this will have a delicious flavour if it is marinated first in a mixture containing strong seasonings like ginger, spring onion and garlic.

Long steaming, with the steamer closed, is ideal for large whole fish, such as sea bass, and for lotus leaf packages or dumplings with a savoury meat-based filling.

Boiling rice
Although in South-East Asia round-grained glutinous rice is often served, long-grain rice cooked until just tender and fluffy, with the grains separate, is equally good and more to Western tastes. Basmati rice has a delicious nutty flavour.

50 g (2 oz) raw rice weight per serving is a good average allowance. 450 g (1 lb) rice would serve 6–8 people generously.

To cook the rice, first rinse it under cold running water and drain. Place the rice in a large, heavy-based saucepan and add about 1¼ times its volume of cold water: 500 ml (18 fl oz) for 450 g (1 lb) rice. Cover the pan with a tight-fitting lid and bring to the boil, then stir the rice, turn down the heat to low and simmer gently for 10 minutes. Turn off the heat under the pan and leave the rice to cook in its own heat for a further 10–12 minutes, until tender.

ROASTING

Most Chinese cooking is done on the top of the stove, and the average Chinese family kitchen is not equipped with an oven. However, it is a popular method of cooking in restaurant kitchens, especially in Peking and Canton, and essential for dishes such as Peking Duck. Chinese roasting is done on a rotisserie or hook in the oven.

DEEP-FRYING

Frying food by immersing it in hot oil is popular with the Chinese, who use their woks for this purpose, although a conventional deep-frier with a wire basket gives equally good results and may be easier for Western cooks to handle. Chopsticks are specially useful for turning the food round in the oil so that it cooks evenly on all sides.

Deep-fried food is deliciously crispy on the outside, with an appetizingly crunchy texture, but remains moist inside, as the sizzling hot oil immediately seals in all the juices. Many foods can be cooked in this way: chicken pieces, pork spare ribs, sliced beef steak, pieces of duck, scallops, prawns in the shell, prawn toasts coated with sesame seeds, cubes of bean curd, dumplings and noodles, and vegetables dipped in batter. Sometimes the food is deep-fried twice, for extra crispness.

A special Chinese deep-frying technique is to fry food wrapped in paper. This is especially popular in Szechuan cuisine. The ingredients are marinated, then wrapped in greaseproof paper or non-stick baking parchment to make small parcels. These are deep-fried so that the contents of the parcels retain all their natural flavours without coming into contact with the oil. The food is served in its paper wrapping.

BRAISING

Larger cuts of meat, whole poultry, etc. benefit from long slow simmering in a sauce. A unique Chinese form of braising is 'red cooking', by which meat is cooked in dark soy sauce, which gives it a reddish-brown colour and a rich flavour. White cooking is used especially for braising leafy vegetables, such as cabbage and Chinese leaves.

ORIENTAL COOKING EQUIPMENT

The equipment used by Chinese cooks is much simpler and more basic than the sophisticated gadgets found in 'Western kitchens – but it is extremely effective! In fact Chinese cooking equipment has mostly remained unchanged in design and use over thousands of years.

In the average Chinese domestic kitchen you would expect to find:
Chopping boards
Cleaver
Wok
Bamboo steamer
Steaming rack

Spatulas
Fish slice
Draining spoon
Metal strainer
Bamboo whisk
Ladle
Granite pestle and mortar

PREPARATION EQUIPMENT

Chopping boards: as chopping and slicing is such an integral part of Oriental food preparation it is essential to have at least one solid wooden chopping board. In fact it is a very good idea to have at least two – a really large one and a smaller one as well. Wooden chopping boards must be kept scrupulously clean and scrubbed after use. Chopping boards with artificial plastic surfaces are not recommended, as they blunt knives and cleavers very quickly.

Cleaver: the Chinese cleaver is quite unlike a Western butcher's meat cleaver in use. It is designed for cutting as well as chopping, and the Chinese use it as Western cooks use a heavy kitchen knife – only the cleaver is much more versatile. Chinese cleavers come in a variety of materials and weights. The best type is of tempered carbon steel, with a wooden handle, of medium weight – light enough to handle easily but heavy enough to give effective results. Contrary, perhaps, to popular belief the Chinese cleaver is easy and safe to use. Use the lighter front half of the blade for slicing and shredding, and the heavier back part for chopping, pounding and tenderizing meat. The flat side of the blade is very useful for lifting quantities of diced, sliced or shredded ingredients.

The cleaver needs to be kept absolutely clean and razor-sharp. Wash and wipe it dry after each use, to prevent rusting and staining. Sharpen it regularly on both sides of the blade and keep it hanging up by the handle on a hook rather than in a kitchen drawer with other utensils, which would dull the metal.

COOKING EQUIPMENT

Wok: this is really indispensable in Chinese cooking – although a frying pan can be used instead for stir-frying, it will not give anything like as good a result. The wok is extremely versatile too, with many uses apart from stir-frying: deep-frying, braising, steaming and boiling.

Woks are traditionally made of iron, which has the advantage of conducting and retaining heat evenly. Stainless steel, copper, and non-stick ceramic enamelled models are also available in the West, but an iron wok, provided it is properly seasoned and cleaned, is undoubtedly the best.

The wok is conical in shape, with a characteristic rounded base. This means that when food is stir-fried it returns automatically to the centre, where the heat is most intense, thus facilitating speedy cooking. The wok may be placed directly over a gas flame; a special adaptor ring will also enable it to be used over an electric hob and has the advantage of keeping it steady as well. Electric plug-in woks are also available, but it is not always easy to control the heat as effectively with these as with the traditional type as electric heat responds less quickly to the control knob.

Woks may be double- or single-handled. A double-handled wok is useful for deep-frying and steaming; a single-handled one is much the best for stir-frying, as it is easy to tilt and shake, and leaves the other hand free for stirring the food in the wok.

Woks come in a variety of sizes, and if you do a good deal of Chinese cooking at home it would be well worth investing in two: a large double-handled one with a lid and a single-handled one measuring about 35 cm (14 inch), offering a good-sized surface area.

Sandpots: these are used by the Chinese

Other equipment might include:
Rice scoop
Wok rack
Clay pots
Cooking chopsticks
Large, deep saucepan
Scraper

Modern equipment: since a flat or apartment is the site of many Oriental cooks' kitchens be they in Singapore or Hong Kong, London or San Francisco, many modern gadgets are appropriate to their lifestyle. Terry Tan may never have persuaded his mother to abandon her pestle and mortar for an electric blender or coffee grinder, but he himself regularly grinds his spices in one. A food processor is also very time-saving for slicing or chopping vegetables and meats neatly and evenly.

GRINDING SPICES

Spices and spice mixtures play an essential role in Oriental cooking. Buying whole spices and grinding them yourself is infinitely preferable to buying powdered spices: grinding releases the volatile oils which convey the spice aroma, so is best done just before use, for the fullest flavour.

A heavy pestle and mortar (ideally made of granite rather than ceramic) is excellent for grinding spices, herbs, garlic, onions and other flavouring ingredients. Spices may also be conveniently ground in a small coffee grinder kept specifically for the purpose.

Oriental spices and flavourings

Cardamom	Sesame seeds
Coriander seeds	Cinnamon
Cumin seeds	Cloves
Fennel seeds	Star anise
Five spice powder	Ginger
Lemon grass	Galangal
Turmeric root	Garlic
Tamarind pods	Chilli peppers
Peppercorns	

for 'clear simmering' – the slow cooking of meats, fish and soups over the lowest possible heat. A suitable alternative for the Western cook would be a heavy-based flameproof casserole used over a very low flame or in a very cool oven.
Electric rice cookers: available here from Oriental cookshops and equipment shops, these cook rice to perfection without requiring any attention from the cook. They are a useful investment for people cooking a lot of rice – and who are not too worried about abandoning the methods of their ancestors or mothers!

SEASONING AND CLEANING A WOK

■ A new iron wok is coated with oil or a wax film to prevent it rusting. This must be removed before use.
■ To do this, heat the wok over high heat until it is very hot indeed, then scrub it in warm soapy water, using a stiff brush. Rinse well.
■ Place the cleaned wok over moderate heat to dry.
■ Now season the wok, to keep it from rusting and to prevent food sticking.
■ To season the wok, wipe the entire surface with a pad of paper towels soaked in cooking oil. The wok is now ready to cook with.
■ After use, wash the wok in hot water but do not use washing-up liquid or other detergents as these will remove the seasoning.
■ Should any food stick to the base of the wok during cooking, brush it off with a stiff brush or non-abrasive scourer.
■ Repeat the seasoning process after use, so that the wok develops a smooth, shiny surface.

PREPARING ORIENTAL FOOD

In Oriental cookery, cutting the ingredients correctly is crucial to the success of a dish. Although the actual cooking may be very brief, preparation can take considerably longer, but is every bit as important as the cooking itself.

Cutting the ingredients properly not only helps bring out their flavour but is also a way of contributing towards the sense of harmony which is all-important in the Oriental attitude towards cooking and life generally. Food is cut into pieces of the same shape and size and thickness to balance each other out in terms of texture and visual appeal as well as to ensure even cooking and easy eating, especially when chopsticks are being used.

There are four basic cutting methods in oriental cooking:

Slicing: meats such as beef or pork, offal, root vegetables, etc. should be cut into thin slices, about the thickness of a piece of card, and about 4 × 1 cm (1½ × ½ inch across), depending on the recipe requirement. Beef steak or liver is easier to

slice wafer-thin if it is cut when it is well chilled or still partially frozen. Meat should be sliced across the grain, as this helps to tenderise it and makes stir-frying easy.

Shredding: an easy way to do this is to stack thin slices of food on top of each other, then cut into thin strips crossways. Meat, root vegetables, ginger root, cucumber, etc. are easy to prepare in this way. The final result is very finely cut foods, ideal for adding to soups, for instance.

Dicing: cut foods like chicken breast fillets, sweet peppers, cakes of bean curd, into long narrow strips, then crossways into small squares. Aim for cubes about 1 cm (½ inch) in size.

Diagonal cutting: carrots, celery sticks, courgettes, cucumber, spring onions, green beans, mangetout, etc. all look especially good if sliced obliquely, to give an attractive slanted shape. To cut diagonally, hold the knife or cleaver at a 45° angle to the vegetables to be cut, with the blade pointing away from you.

However the ingredients for a meal are cut, they should always be prepared before starting to cook and put to one side, each ingredient in its own dish, until needed. Foods which require the longest cooking will, obviously, be put into the wok or saucepan first, with the others being added in their turn.

CLEANING SQUID

Squid is a popular fish in oriental cooking. Squid rings keep their shape well and are especially delicious deep-fried, or in a stir-fried dish. Only the tentacles and body of the squid are eaten. In this book, you will find them used in soup – see Stuffed Squid Soup (page 14) – as well as fish and noodle dishes.

Once the squid has been cleaned (as in the two diagrams, right) it may be used whole (but sever the tentacles from the head), or the body sac may be cut into rings, using a Chinese cleaver or sharp kitchen knife.

1. To remove the quill or pen from squid, draw back the rim of the body sac to reveal the quill inside. Grasp the quill by the tip and gently pull it free of the surrounding flesh.

2. Hold the body sac in one hand and grasp the head just below the eyes with the other. Gently pull the head from the body. Pull the mucous membrane from the body.

BONING A DUCK OR CHICKEN

A whole boned duck or chicken may be stuffed and roasted, when it will look like the complete bird, or cut into shreds, strips or slices, as in several recipes in this book.

While a duck was used to illustrate the boning process in this sequence of pictures, the basic method may be applied to other birds, such as chicken or even goose. The goose photographed on page 81 (Eight-treasure roast goose) was boned following this method.

1. Cut the neck skin off to within an inch or so of the body, using kitchen scissors or a sharp knife.

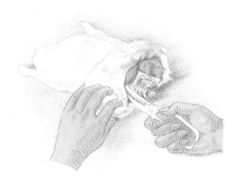

2. Folding the remaining skin as far back as it will go and, with tiny snips, free the meat around the neck cavity.

3. Wiggle each wing to find the joint where it meets the carcass, then cut through to detach the wing intact.

4. Continue to free the meat from the carcass with tiny snips, turning the bird over and rolling the skin back.

5. Free the meat and cut the joints to detach the leg bones from the carcass to leave the leg itself intact.

should look like a flattened bird, with the leg bone and the wing bone still intact. Properly stuffed (recipes will give required quantities), the bird will plump up again to its true size during cooking. Use the carcase, cut-away bones etc, to make stock for soups and other dishes.

6. Cut the meat away from the rest of the carcass, always cutting as close to the bone as you can. Try not to pierce the outside skin.

7. Cut through the joint where the tail bone is attached to the backbone, leaving the tail with skin and meat. Then turn the skin of the now boned bird right side out again. It

GARNISHING ORIENTAL FOOD

Fresh herbs – sprigs or individual leaves, whole or chopped – make attractive and appropriate garnishes for Oriental food, as well as lending it flavour. Coriander, sweet basil, mint and lemon grass are good.

Edible flowers also look very pretty: in South-East Asia pink ginger flowers are often used as a garnish; in the West mauve chive flowers might be used instead. Nasturtium flowers would lend brilliant colour to a pale dish, and small chrysanthemums would look stunning as a garnish for dinner party fare.

It is also nice to use fresh vegetables for garnishing. Something as simple as a sprinkling of finely chopped spring onion, or thinly shaved carrot ribbons gives a special touch to a dish. More elaborate garnishes for Oriental food could include radish roses, spring onion tassels and celery and red pepper bundles.

SPRING ONION TASSELS

1. Cut the white bulbs from the spring onions and reserve for another use. Trim away enough of the green stalk to make a total length of about 7.5 cm (3 inch). Remove the thin papery membrane and any discoloured or damaged outside leaves.

2. Cut lengthways through the stalk several times to within about 3.5 cm (1½ inch) of the end of the white part.

3. Immerse the spring onion tassels in a bowl of iced water and leave for 1 hour until they have opened out.

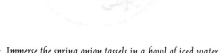

CELERY AND RED PEPPER BUNDLES

1. Trim and wash a celery stick and cut it into 5 cm (2 inch) lengths. Cut the celery into very thin strips, about half the width of a matchstick.

2. Seed half a large red pepper and remove all the white membrane. Cut the flesh into long thin strips.

3. Blanch in boiling water for 1 minute, to retain the colour and make the pepper more pliable, then drain and pat dry carefully.

4. Take a bundle of celery strips and carefully tie round with a red pepper strip, to hold the celery strips together. This amount of celery and red pepper should make 3–4 bundles.

USING CHOPSTICKS

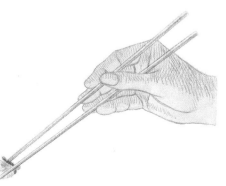

RADISH ROSES

1. Wash and trim the radishes.

2. For each radish, cut a row of petal shapes near the base, keeping them joined to the radish at the base of the 'petal'.

3. Cut more rows of petals in between and above the first row until you reach the top of the radish.

4. Place in iced water for several hours to open out.

Hold the chopsticks between the thumb and fingers, slightly over halfway down. Bring the chopsticks together in a gentle pincer movement, to grip the food securely.

Once you have become dexterous in handling chopsticks you will find them very useful for serving as well as eating food, and as a cooking implement, especially for turning ingredients in a marinade or when stir-frying.

ENTERTAINING ORIENTAL STYLE

Oriental cuisine offers plenty of scope for different styles of entertaining, from a large dinner party or buffet to a quickly prepared impromptu supper.

The way Chinese food is traditionally served itself creates a very pleasant informal and relaxed atmosphere at a party. Guests are seated at a round table with the dishes grouped in the centre so that everyone can share the food and help themselves and others to it. A Chinese meal involves no carving or 'dishing up'; instead, the food is all in bite-sized pieces, for easy serving and eating.

Although in Malaysia and Indonesia food is usually eaten from a plate with a spoon and fork, the Chinese eat from individual bowls set on medium-sized plates, and they use chopsticks to eat with. It is very well worth mastering the art of chopsticks, which is really very easy once you know how! However, you can always set the table with spoons and forks as well, to ensure that less confident guests will enjoy their meal.

Chinese eating bowls double as soup bowls as well, in which case porcelain spoons are used to eat the soup. So a Chinese meal involves minimal washing up, which can be a real boon for the hostess at the end of an enjoyable evening.

Planning the menu carefully is an important aspect of any successful Chinese meal, which does not follow the Western order of soup or starter, main course, pudding. At a casual supper for a small number of people all the dishes might be placed on the table simultaneously. At a larger dinner the natural sequence would be to progress from cold to hot dishes, from quick dishes such as stir-fries to ones that take longer, like braised dishes, and from lighter to rich food. A typical order might be:

1st course: cold starter dishes or Oriental salads, sliced or shredded meats, etc.
2nd course: some hot starter vegetable and seafood dishes.
3rd course: a rich, substantial soup.
Main course: the principal dishes, such as a whole steamed fish and braised joint of pork.
Final course: fruit, sweets, dim sum snacks.

Whether the meal is very simple or more formal, the idea behind it is the same: the various dishes should be well balanced within themselves and in conjunction with each other, to create the overall sense of harmony that is the ultimate goal of the Chinese way of life. The various dishes should centre round a number of different main ingredients, and duplication should be avoided: one beef or pork dish, one chicken dish, one dish of fish or seafood, and so on. Achieving pleasing contrasts in terms of taste, colour and texture is very important to the Chinese. The following typical combinations give an idea of how this might work:

■ A dish of succulent pink prawns and crisp, bright green mangetout
■ A dish of tender diced chicken with crunchy cashew nuts
■ A dish of rich brown beef cut into meltingly tender strips, with crisp strips of carrot or red pepper.

At a formal Chinese dinner the dishes would be chosen to feature as many different cooking styles as possible – steaming, stir-frying, braising and so on, but each style would be illustrated by just one dish. The number of dishes would also be even, e.g. 8, 10 or 12, and so on, again to create a sense of balance.

When calculating the number of dishes to serve, it is almost as difficult to be precise as it is to give exact quantities and cooking times in Chinese recipes: it is all very much a matter of judgement based on experience. However, as a rough guide one might allow one main dish per person, always remembering that this does not mean that one person will eat just one complete dish: the whole idea of a Chinese meal is that all the dishes should be shared.

Puddings and desserts are not traditionally served at the end of a meal, as in the West. However, a selection of Chinese desserts is given on pages 00–0, which would satisfy even the sweetest tooth. Or you could round off the meal with some fresh exotic fruit, such as mango or lychees. One excellent Szechuan restaurant in London serves an attractive platter of sliced oranges at the end of the meal.

Contrary to popular belief, in China tea is not traditionally drunk throughout the meal, but usually before or after. Between the courses the Chinese like to drink a light soup, which can be a very simple clear broth based on a well-flavoured meat or vegetable stock. If you are offering tea, there is a wide selection at any Chinese supermarket or food store, as literally hundreds of varieties grow in China, falling into two main categories: unfermented green tea and fermented black. Fragrant jasmine tea is a very popular choice in the West. Serving the tea from an oriental bamboo-handled tea pot in tiny bowls would give your Chinese meal a nice authentic touch.

Dry to medium white wine, and light fruity red wine both go very well with Chinese food. French Muscadet or Sauvignon, Californian Chardonnay or German Riesling or Moselle would be a good choice of whites, and among the reds a young Beaujolais, or a Spanish Rioja or Australian Cabernet Sauvignon.

MENU PLANNER

A CHINESE FEAST

Pearl River (South China) salad: page 27

Crispy prawn balls: page 96

Spare ribs in capital sauce: page 50

Hot and sour sliced liver soup with bean curd: page 8

Steamed sea bass: page 86

Braised quail with ginger wine: page 72

Stir-fried broccoli with Chinese dried shrimps
and fried mushrooms: page 20

Eight-treasure glutinous rice: page 108

Petite pineapples: page 121

LIGHT LUNCHES

Quick-fried slivers of chicken with asparagus: page 60

Singapore noodles: page 102

Tianjin (North China) salad: page 23

Mee Goreng: page 102

Stuffed courgettes: page 28

Mushroom noodles: page 107

Onion and ham omelette: page 34

Yangtze (East China) salad: page 24

Fish wrapped in lotus leaves: page 96

Quick-fried diced chicken and mushrooms
with chicken liver and cucumber: page 62

BARBECUE

Spicy spare ribs: page 50

Prawn satay with peanut sauce: page 92

Yogurt lamb chops: page 49

Tropical fruit punch: page 124

INFORMAL SUPPERS

Quick-fried beef ribbons with shredded ginger,
carrot and spring onion: page 38

Stir-fried chicken with walnuts: page 72

Steamed scallops in black bean sauce: page 95

Fresh and dried shrimp soup with spinach
and bean curd: page 10

Mixed spice rice: page 110

———————

Cinnamon beef: page 43

Spicy sesame-braised fish: page 89

Szechuan quick-fried ribbon of duck with shredded ginger
in hot black bean sauce: page 77

Chinese cabbage with white fu-yung sauce: page 19

Boiled rice

MEAT-FREE MEALS

Aubergine starters: page 31

Vegetarian chow mein: page 101

Peking toffee apples: page 116

———————

Tropical great salad: page 34

Mixed vegetable curry: page 31

Lotus seed pudding: page 124

———————

Spicy Okra: page 28

Beggar's noodles: page 104

Sticky rice cake: page 118

INDEX

ACKNOWLEDGEMENTS

Photography
DAVID JOHNSON

Photographic styling
MARIAN PRICE

Preparation of food for photography
JENNY SHAPTER

Illustrations
LINDA SMITH

Step-by-step illustrations
PATRICIA CAPON

Map illustration
EUGENE FLEURY

Cover photography
VERNON MORGAN

Preparation of food for cover photography
ALLYSON BIRCH